Tokyo

W9-AEB-643

Initially arriving in Japan in 1999 to teach English for a year, **Rob Goss** has ended up staying far longer than planned without really understanding why. Cupid's arrow certainly played a part, as did the pitter-patter of part-Japanese, part-British baby feet that followed. Living in a city that never ceases to amaze helps too. Then there's having a job he loves—writing about Japan for magazines such as *Time* and *National Geographic Traveler*, and, at latest count, for some 70 other magazines, book publishers and newspapers around the globe. Rob is also the author of the award-winning *Tuttle Travel Pack Japan*, recipient of a Gold Prize at the 2013 North American Travel Journalist Association Awards.

Published by Tuttle Publishing, an imprint of Periplus Editions (HK) Ltd

www.tuttlepublishing.com

Copyright © 2014 Periplus Editions (HK) Ltd
(Refer to Photo Credits page for photos ©)

All rights reserved. No part of this publication may be reproduced or utilized in any form or by any means, electronic or mechanical, including photocopying, recording, or by any information storage and retrieval system, without prior written permission from the publisher.

ISBN: 978-4-8053-1066-3

Distributed by

North America, Latin America & Europe
Tuttle Publishing
364 Innovation Drive
North Clarendon, VT 05759-9436 U.S.A.
Tel: 1 (802) 773-8930
Fax: 1 (802) 773-6993
info@tuttlepublishing.com
www.tuttlepublishing.com

Japan
Tuttle Publishing
Yaekari Building, 3rd Floor
5-4-12 Osaki, Shinagawa-ku
Tokyo 141-0032
Tel: (81) 3 5437-0171
Fax: (81) 3 5437-0755
sales@tuttle.co.jp
www.tuttle.co.jp

Asia Pacific
Berkeley Books Pte. Ltd.
61 Tai Seng Avenue, #02-12
Singapore 534167
Tel: (65) 6280-1330
Fax: (65) 6280-6290
inquiries@periplus.com.sg
www.periplus.com

16 15 14   10 9 8 7 6 5 4 3 2 1

Printed in Singapore   1408CP

TUTTLE PUBLISHING® is a registered trademark of Tuttle Publishing, a division of Periplus Editions (HK) Ltd.

LONGWOOD PUBLIC LIBRARY

TUTTLE TRAVEL PACK

TOKYO

Rob Goss

TUTTLE Publishing

Tokyo │ Rutland, Vermont │ Singapore

BACK TO THE FUTURE

Before I came to Tokyo, all I knew of Japan were stereotypical images of geisha and sumo, of packed commuter trains and city streets drenched in neon, of overworked and overly formal *sarariman* (salaryman). Eyes wide in the awe of discovering a new city, Tokyo didn't disappoint. The first time I had to squeeze onto a rush-hour train was chaos, elbows flying and umbrellas swishing around like modern-day samurai swords. A few days later, my first encounter with Shinjuku was like being thrown into a future dreamed up by Isaac Asimov or Philip K. Dick. There were flashing lights, buildings blocking out the sky, sirens, shoulder bumps from the crowds, and blasts of noise and air-conditioning from every shop front I passed. Everything was new. Most things were incomprehensible. I'd become illiterate overnight. It was fantastic.

Once the initial shock and awe had begun to subside, however, it wasn't long before I started to find that there was so much more to Japan than I'd seen in guidebooks and travel documentaries. Yes, the Japanese bow, but they don't spend half their time doing it. And yes, they eat raw fish, but it's only a small part of a marvelous and varied culinary heritage. Despite the high-rise, neon-lit images in guidebooks, for most Japanese this is a country of low-rise suburbs and rural communities. For all the talk of Japanese as staid and reserved, spend a night in a local *izakaya* (pub-cum-restaurant) and you'll soon learn they can crack a risqué joke as well as anybody. If there's anything I've learned in over a decade in Tokyo, it's that there's a lot more to almost every aspect of Japan and Tokyo than initially meets the eye. I hope this book will you help discover that there's more to Japan and its capital, too. Happy travels!

CONTENTS

Tokyo at a Glance

Geography

Situated in the center of the Kanto region, on the eastern side of Japan's main island Honshu, Tokyo's core is comprised of 23 *ku* (wards), with another 39 municipalities (*shi*) to the west of these. There are also two island chains that fall under Tokyo's jurisdiction, the Izu Islands and the Ogawasara Islands, the latter lying 1,000 km (620 miles) south of Tokyo.

Climate

In winter, Tokyo tends to be quite dry and mild (and very often sunny), with the temperature rarely dropping below 0 °C and often in excess of 10 °C. Spring is heralded by a pink front of cherry blossom in late March and early April, signaling the arrival of pleasantly warm temperatures that will last through May (and the arrival of cedar pollen that has some 20% of Tokyoites watery eyed hiding behind surgical masks). Separating spring from summer is a three- to four-week rainy season in June, during which the heat and humidity start to rise and the skies remain mostly grey.

From July the rain gives way to clear summer skies—occasionally punctuated by a typhoon—that last through to late September. Summer high temperatures are typically around 32 °C–35 °C with midnight lows around the 25 °C mark, and the humidity can be extremely oppressive. After several months of sweating and *natsu bate* (summer fatigue), the temperatures begin to drop with the start of autumn in October. It's a wonderful time to visit Japan as the skies stay clear, the air feels fresh again and for a couple of months the high temperature hovers in the low to mid-20 °C.

People

At last count, Tokyo's population was 13.2 million, representing just over 10% of the population of the entire country. Some 35 million people live in the Greater Tokyo area, which is comprised of Tokyo and the neighboring prefectures of Chiba, Kanagawa and Saitama. Although Tokyo's population has been rising since the end of World War II, when it had fallen to 3.5 million, that growth isn't expected to last. According to the most recent national census, Japan's declining birth rate could see Tokyo's population drop under 12 million by 2050 and under 8 million by 2100.

Language

The official language of Japan is Japanese (apologies for stating the painfully obvious) and is the first language of 99% of the Japanese population. Besides Japanese, Okinawa in the far south also has its own related but minor Ryukyuan languages, while the indigenous Ainu people of Hokkaido in the far north have the unrelated Ainu language. With three

Modern Tokyo still has some traditional houses

Tokyo Tower, one of the city's most distinctive landmarks, sharing the skyline with the towers of Roppongi (left).

separate writing systems (the complicated kanji and the easier phonetic hiragana and katakana) which between them use thousands of different characters, not to mention a complex system of honorifics, Japanese isn't the easiest language to quickly get to grips with. That said, in central Tokyo and the main tourist areas you will easily be able to get by in English. If you'd like to try speaking a bit of Japanese (and it will be appreciated), have a look at the section on useful expressions and pronunciation on pages 89–91.

Religion

The Japanese typically say they are born Shinto but die Buddhist, in reference to the traditional rituals used for birth and death. In fact, they don't really consider themselves to be religious at all; more than 80% say they have no religious affiliation and 65% don't believe in God or Buddha. Instead, you can think of Buddhism, which arrived from China in the 6th century, and Shinto, the indigenous religion of Japan, effectively forming one set of traditional practices that are followed by the majority. Just over 80% say they practice traditions related to Shintoism, while approximately 70% practice those related to Buddhism.

Government

Japan is a parliamentary government with a constitutional monarchy, the current constitution having been adopted in 1947. Emperor Akihito is the chief of state, while the head of state is the prime minister, as of writing Shinzo Abe, although with the rate Japan goes through prime ministers this could have changed several times by the time you read this! The legislative branch of government, the Diet, consists of a 242-member House of Councilors and a 450-member House of Representatives. The prime minister is designated by the Diet and is usually the leader of the majority party or majority coalition in the House of Representatives.

Sanja Matsuri, Asakusa

Tuttle Travel Pack Tokyo
HOW TO USE THIS BOOK

Packed with up-to-date, thoroughly researched information written by locals, the Tuttle series of Travel Packs are indispensable companions on your global travels. The portable size and straightforward format make them easy to use for everyone, no matter if you're a regular or first-time visitor to the city.

In the front of the book, we give you a brief overview of Tokyo, taking a look at its people, language and climate, then Chapter 1 covers Tokyo's 'Don't Miss' Sights, detailing the top 13 places to visit and things to do—from taking in the frenetic early morning auctions at Tsukiji Fish Market and exploring the modern Roppongi Hills and Tokyo Midtown complexes to soaking in the hot spring baths at Oedo Onsen Monogatari and hiking up Mount Takao.

In Chapter 2, we take a more detailed look at the incredibly varied neighborhoods that make up Tokyo, starting with a day out that takes in the upmarket Ginza district and nearby Imperial Palace and ending up with a day on the family-friendly man-made island of Odaiba in Tokyo Bay. In between, we go from the chic Omotesando-dori and youthful Shibuya to the more traditional Asakusa and Yanesen districts, and more. We also explore several not-to-miss areas within day-trip range of Tokyo, including the ancient shrines and temples of Kamakura, the lavish Tosho-gu Shrine in Nikko and the popular hot spring resort of Hakone.

In Chapter 3: Author's Recommendations, our Tokyo-based author makes his picks for the city's best hotels and restaurants, top kid-friendly activities, best places to shop, must-see galleries and museums, and more. Lastly, the Travel Facts section presents all you need to know before you go, including the low-down on visas, health and safety advice, important points of etiquette, useful Japanese and a lot more to help take the stress out of your time in the world's most mesmerizing capital.

While all information is correct at time of print, do make sure to check ahead if you plan to visit any of the venues listed within, as places tend to frequently open and close, especially in a city that has a history of transforming itself as often and rapidly as Tokyo. As such, the publisher cannot accept responsibility for any errors that may be contained within the Travel Pack.

CHAPTER 1
TOKYO'S
'Don't Miss' Sights

Tokyo Skytree towers above eastern Tokyo

Observation deck at Roppongi Hills

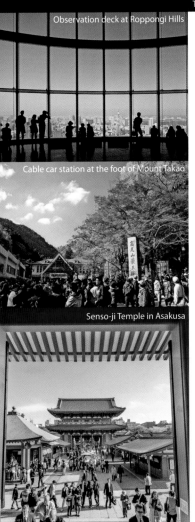

Cable car station at the foot of Mount Takao

Senso-ji Temple in Asakusa

Whether discovering historic temples or finding yourself hopelessly lost in translation, Tokyo offers visitors an unforgettable range of experiences and sights. The 13 listings that follow is my own selection of Tokyo's 'Don't Miss' Sights, chosen to provide a taste of all the components that come together to make a trip to Japan's capital so memorable.

1   Meiji Jingu Shrine
2   Omotesanda Shopping Avenue
3   Tsukiji Fish Market
4   Tokyo Skytree
5   Senso-ji Temple in Asakusa
6   Sumida River Cruise
7   A Stroll Through the Yanaka District
8   Akihabara
9   Edo-Tokyo History Museum
10 Roppongi Hills and Tokyo Midtown
11 A Visit to Oedo Hot Springs in Odaiba
12 Shinjuku Gyoen Park
13 A Hike Up Mount Takao

MAKING THE MOST OF YOUR VISIT

With so many things to see and do, knowing where to start and what to explore in Tokyo is no easy task. So what to do? You could stare down jetlag on your first day by getting up bright and early for the **Tsukiji Fish Market** (page 11) where the frenetic early morning tuna auction should jolt you into life. After a *sushi* breakfast at the market, take to the streets of nearby Ginza for its famed department stores and boutiques, and then stroll over to the Imperial Palace (page 26) to catch a glimpse of the off-limits palace buildings and wander its landscaped outer gardens.

On your second day, you could explore the city's old east side, starting with Senso-ji Temple in Asakusa (page 13) before browsing the culinary ware stores of nearby Kappabashi (page 72). Alternatively, soak up the east-side vibe with a trip to the Ueno district (page 33) for the lively Ameyoko street market, several of the city's best museums, and some down time in Ueno Park before a couple of hours strolling around the narrow, winding back streets of Yanaka, Nezu and Sendagi (collectively known as Yanesen, page 15)—an older, more down-to-earth side of Tokyo that belies the city's hectic, neon-drenched image.

On your third day, immerse yourself in central Tokyo with a stroll among the fashion-conscious throngs of Omotesando-dori and the teenyboppers of Harajuku and Shibuya, on the way stopping at the magnificent Meiji Jingu Shrine (page 9). Another day could be spent first browsing the electronics and geeky (*otaku*) stores in Akihabara (page 36), then plunging into the crowded streets of Shinjuku (page 37)—the epitome of brash, modern Tokyo—or the more stylish Roppongi Hills and Tokyo Midtown urban develop-ments in Roppongi (page 18).

For a fun family day out, look no further than Odaiba (page 42). With attractions that include the Oedo Onsen baths (page 19), one of the coolest science museum's kids will get to see (page 73) and arguably Japan's most mind-blowing amusement arcade (Joypolis, page 74), the man-made island has enough to keep adults and kids of all ages happy until well past bedtime. Alternatively, you could brave the crowds and head east of Tokyo to the Tokyo Disney Resort (page 74).

As well as exploring Tokyo, also try to get out of the capital and discover some of the spectacular historical and natural sites on its doorstep. Even just a day trip out of Tokyo will give you a whole new perspective on Japan. If time is limited, get up early and have a day trip to Kamakura (page 44), the 13th-century capital, to take in the Daibutsu (Great Statue of Buddha) at Hase's Kotoku-in Temple (page 44) and many other ancient sites. If you prefer a taste of nature, head an hour west of Shinjuku and hike up Mount Takao (page 21).

If you can spare a night away from Tokyo, catch a train a couple of hours north to the World Heritage Tosho-gu shrine in Nikko (page 51), the outrageously lavish complex built by Tokugawa Ieyasu, the first shogun of the Edo era (1603–1868). You could do this as a long day trip, but it's far better to slowly explore Nikko's temples and shrines and still have time to take in the nearby Kegon Waterfalls and Lake Chuzenji (page 53). Better still, that will give you the opportunity to stay in one of Nikko's traditional inns (*ryokan*). For an alternative place to try a *ryokan*, head just under two hours west to Hakone (page 54) for a soak in one of the area's many natural outdoor hot springs and for superb views of majestic Mount Fuji (page 55).

1 Meiji Jingu Shrine
Tradition and tranquility amid the urban sprawl

Dedicated to the souls of the Emperor Meiji, the man who lead Japan's transition from feudal state to modern world power in the late 19th and early 20th centuries, and his consort Empress Shoken, the quiet hush and calm of Meiji Jingu Shrine and its inner precinct (the Naien) is a perfect example of the contrasts that have come to define Tokyo—of the modern city standing at ease alongside the old city and its enduring traditions. In Meiji Jingu's case, this enclave of "old Japan" rubs shoulders with the youthful, anything-goes Harajuku area and cosmopolitan Omotesando-dori.

After passing under the first of Meiji Jingu's three grand *torii* gateways, walking along gravel pathways shaded by the towering forest that enshrouds the main shrine, it's hard to believe all this (shrine and 28-hectare/70-acre forest) was built only after the emperor's death in 1912, construction eventually finishing in the fall of 1920. In fact, the buildings that are here now date only to the late 1950s when they were rebuilt after being leveled in the air raids that destroyed so much of Tokyo in 1945. Yet, regardless of age, the inner precinct is undoubtedly ancient in

manner. On one visit you might see a Shinto wedding procession gracefully moving through the grounds. On another you will see people writing wishes on wood plaques and hanging them on racks in front of the main shrine, where people bow to pray, only their gentle ritual hand claps punctuating the silence.

Not surprisingly in this city of contrasts, Meiji Jingu's outer precinct (the Gaien) couldn't be more different to the tranquil inner. Stretching over 32 hectares (80 acres), the Gaien is home to parkland and an incredible array of sports facilities, including the 48,000-seat National Stadium, the main venue for the 1964 Tokyo Olympics. The International Olympic Committee is always keen to talk about the "Olympic legacy" the games leave in each host city, and with the Gaien they have a legacy that—like the shrine itself—has managed to stand the test of time.

Opening Times The main shrine is open daily from sunrise to sunset. **Getting There** A several-minute walk from either Harajuku Station on the Yamanote Line or Meiji Jingumae on the Chiyoda Line. **Contact** Meiji Jingu Shrine: www.meijijingu.or.jp. Gaien: www.meijijingugaien.jp. **Admission Fee** Meiji Jingu Shrine is free.

2 Omotesando Shopping Avenue
Tokyo's chicest street is defined by high fashion

If you had to pick one place that best encapsulates "chic Tokyo", this 800-meter (2,625-foot)-long zelkova-lined boulevard and the side streets that wind off of it would have to be it. Although it was originally created as an approach to Meiji Jingu Shrine (page 9) in the Taisho era (1912–26), Omotesando-dori has become synonymous in recent years with two things: high-end shopping and modern architecture.

The area is home to the flagship stores of brands like Louis Vuitton, Prada and Dior as well as architectural master-pieces such as Tod's, a slim, L-shaped building encased in an enclosure of sharply angled concrete elements and polygonal glass plates that was designed by 2013 Pritzker Prize winner Toyo Ito. Then there's Omotesando's centerpiece, Omotesando Hills, which transformed the street when it opened in 2006. Designed by acclaimed architect Tadao Ando, the 250-meter (820-foot)-long mall runs along a quarter of Omotesando-dori's length. Some 100 shops and restaurants as well as 38 luxury apartments are housed on the inside, which is defined by a six-level atrium stretching three stories above ground and three below, with a spiraling ramp connecting the different levels.

Not that all the shops along Omotesando-dori fall in the high-end or high-style bracket. Opposite Omotesando Hills is the fantastic Oriental Bazaar (page 72), a one-stop shop for almost every conceivable souvenir, from "I Love Tokyo" T-shirts to beautiful used kimono and even fine antique furniture. On a street known for its cutting-edge archi-tecture, you've got to applaud the brash-ness of the bazaar's faux oriental temple façade, which looks like something trans-planted straight from ancient China. Like the many other mismatched buildings in Tokyo, it poses the question: just who is in charge of planning permits?

Getting There Omotesando-dori can be accessed at one end by Omotesando Station on the Chiyoda, Ginza and Hanzomon subway lines, and the other by Meiji Jingumae Station on the Chiyoda Line and Harajuku Station on the JR Yamanote Line.

3 Tsukiji Fish Market
Get up early for lively auctions and a fine sushi breakfast

I wonder what the original fishermen of Tsukiji would make of the giant wholesale market that now dominates the Tsukiji area. When the first Edo-era shogun, Tokugawa Ieyasu, brought fishermen in from Osaka at the start of the 17th century to supply his new capital with seafood, the area was no more than mudflats. It wasn't until the Great Kanto Earthquake of 1923, after which Tokyo's small private markets were consolidated into large wholesale venues, that Tsukiji took its current form—and what a form!

Today, Tsukiji is home to more than 60,000 wholesalers, buyers and shippers supplying Tokyo's restaurants and shops with what amounts to more than 700,000 tons of seafood a year. To give that some financial context, each day more than ¥1.5 billion ($15 million) worth of produce is traded here, and not only seafood. To a lesser extent, Tsukiji also trades in vegetables, meat, and even cooking utensils, while the outer part of the market houses numerous small *sushi* bars (I recommend **Ryuzushi** in Building No. 1, which is open from 6.30 a.m.).

Now for the bad news. Although the outer market is great to visit any time before lunch, to see Tsukiji at its best you really need to get there very early. At just before 5.30 a.m. the market bursts into life with the ringing of a bell that heralds the start of the daily tuna auctions in a cavernous warehouse filled with rows of frozen tuna. What follows is a blur of hand signals set to a cacophony of hollers—a rapid to and fro between auctioneer and wholesalers that's incomprehensible to the outsider. It's like watching a classical performance but with choreographed Kabuki moves and kimono replaced by rubber boots and overalls. More bad news. The tuna auctions are limited to 120 people on a first-come basis, with registration starting at 5 a.m. To guarantee a place, be in line by an ungodly 4 a.m. at the latest.

Opening Times 5 a.m.–3 p.m. Closed Sun and 2nd/4th Weds. **Getting There** Tsukiji Market is a short walk from either Tsukiji Shijo Station on the Oedo subway line or Tsukiji Station on the Hibiya subway line. **Contact** www.tsukiji-market.or.jp **Admission Fee** Free.

4 Tokyo Skytree
Tokyo's newest landmark dominates the eastern skyline

You can't spend a day in eastern Tokyo without catching at least a few glimpses of the most recent high-rise addition to the city's skyline. When I walk to my local shops, almost 10 km (6 miles) from the Skytree, its white metallic lattice frame (officially dubbed "Skytree white") is always there in the distance, sometimes piercing a bright blue sky, sometimes partially visible through gray cloud. Take an evening run along the Arakawa River and it's my constant companion to the west, its purple and gold or pale blue illuminations flickering above the rest of the cityscape like the lights of a hovering spaceship.

Opened in 2012 after four years of construction, Tokyo Skytree was built by Tobu Railway and a group of six terrestrial broadcasters in part to relay radio and television broadcast signals and in part to be the centerpiece of a commercial development comprising several buildings that combine restaurants, vertigo-inducing observation decks, amusement facilities, such as an aquarium, and office spaces. It also ended up

becoming one of Tokyo's biggest tourist attractions, with some 1.6 million people visiting in its first week of business.

Part of the attraction is the height. At 634 meters (2,000 feet), the Skytree isn't just the tallest structure in Japan, it's the tallest tower in the world and the second tallest structure of any kind in the world after the 830-meter (1,900-foot) Burj Khalifa in Dubai. The potential for sweaty palms and dizziness aside, the 360-degree views from the two observation decks, 350 meters (800 feet) and 450 meters (1,4675 feet) up, are mesmerizing, with Tokyo transformed into an incredibly detailed moving diorama far below.

Opening Times Open daily 8 a.m.–10 p.m.
Getting There From Asakusa Station, take the Tobu Skytree Line one stop to Tokyo Skytree Station. Alternatively, it's a 15-minute walk from Asakusa. Also accessible via Oshiage Station on the Hanzomon Line. **Contact** www.tokyo-skytree.jp
Admission Fee 350 m observation deck, ¥2,000 (¥2,500 for a reserved day/time ticket to avoid the queues, which can be hours long); additional ¥1,000 to then go to the 450 m deck. Cheaper tickets are available for children of various ages.

5 Senso-ji Temple in Asakusa
Tokyo's most venerable and colorful Buddhist temple

According to legend, there has been a temple in Asakusa since the 620s when two brothers caught a golden image of Kannon, the goddess of mercy, in their nets while fishing in the nearby Sumida River. Awestruck by the tiny statue offered up by the water, the story goes that they were inspired to build a temple in which to enshrine it.

To be fair, the temple nowadays splits opinion. For some people it's become a bit of a tourist trap, for others it's still one of Tokyo's best attractions. If you ask me, it can be both. Nakamise-dori, the vibrant shop-lined street that forms the main approach to Senso-ji, in places is as touristy as it gets in Tokyo, with its plastic samurai swords and slow-moving horde of tourists. The rest of the Senso-ji Temple complex is simply magnificent.

Senso-ji greets visitors with the mighty Kaminari-mon (Thunder Gate), a roofed gate standing almost 12 meters (39 feet) high and 12 meters wide under which hangs a 680-kilogram (1,500-pound) red paper lantern. Protected on either side by the menacing bronze statues of Raijin and Fujin, the gods of thunder and wind, Kaminari-mon is merely a taste of what's to come. At the other end of Nakamise-dori, the two-story Hozomon Gate stands 22 meters (72 feet) high and is decorated with three giant lanterns and two 362-kilogram (800-pound) straw sandals. Used to store many of Senso-ji's most precious relics, it is guarded by two grim-faced 5-meter (16-foot)-tall statues of Nio, the guardian deity of the Buddha. Beyond that, in air heavy with pungent incense, comes a five-tiered pagoda and the larger, albeit less ornate, main building, in front of which visitors pray and wave incense smoke over themselves for its supposed curative powers.

I'm not sold on the curative effects of smoke but I am sold on Senso-ji. In the middle of a city as modern and cramped as Tokyo, it's an incredible combination of tradition and scale.

Opening Times Open 24/7. **Getting There** Senso-ji is a several-minute walk from Asakusa on the Asakusa and Ginza subway lines. **Contact** www.senso-ji.jp. **Admission Fee** Free.

6 Sumida River Cruise
Take to the water for a different perspective on the city

A journey down the Sumida River from Asakusa takes you close to both Tokyo's past and the different faces of its present. The city's expansive but often overlooked waterways were once crucial commercial arteries that helped drive the city's growth, and today you'll still see giant barges plying the waters carrying industrial material. At night, you'll also see the orange lanterns of traditional *yakatabune* houseboats heading up and down the rivers, nowadays carrying drinkers and diners on party cruises.

As you leave Asakusa and head south down the Sumida, the Skytree gradually shrinking in the distance behind you, the river begins to offer views of everyday Tokyo that you won't find by wandering the streets of Ginza or Roppongi. There will be the occasional angler fishing from the concrete river bank and ageing gray apartment blocks accented by futons hung out on balconies to air—some being beaten to purge the dust mites. Every so often you'll see a cluster of makeshift cardboard homes covered by blue tarpaulins to keep out the rain, and then

enclaves of glistening high-rise, high-rent apartments that are home to more fortunate waterside residents.

For an additional ¥300 on the fare, the journey is even better if you rent one of the English audio guides that give an insightful commentary on the history of Tokyo and sights along the river. Also think about which route you want to take. There are quite a few available, all going down the Sumida River and then heading off to different parts of Tokyo Bay, but the best two for combining with other attractions are the 35-minute direct route from Asakusa to the Hama-Rikyu Gardens (page 77) and the 70-minute Asakusa to Odaiba route (see page 32) that requires a transfer at Hinode Pier.

Opening Times The first boat of the day leaves Asakusa at 9.50 a.m. They then run once or twice an hour until around 7 p.m. See the website below for timetables. **Getting There** The Asakusa pier is a one-minute walk from Asakusa subway station. **Contact** www.suijobus.co.jp (mostly in Japanese, but with some English). **Admission Fee** Asakusa direct to Hama-Rikyu (¥760), Asakusa to Odaiba via Hinode (¥1,220).

7 A Stroll Through the Yanaka District
Discover "Old Tokyo" in this eastside village neighborhood

Yanaka, one of three adjoining neighborhoods that together make up the area known as Yanesen (Yanaka, Nezu and Sendagi; see pull-out map K2), was best described by noted American writer Donald Richie when he called it "One of the best preserved sections of village-Tokyo." As Richie explains in his book *Tokyo Megacity*, Yanaka owes its preservation to having somehow avoided both the devastation of the 1923 Great Kanto Earthquake and the fire-bombing of Tokyo in 1945. If you want to feel "old Tokyo", then it's Yanaka you need to visit.

Walk down Yanaka's main shopping street, Yanaka Ginza, and you will find it lined with open-fronted mom-and-pop stores and small restaurants, ranging from Hatsuneya at the far end of the street, which sells traditional textiles and clothing, to the fine teas at Kaneyoshien halfway up and the hand-made candies at Goto no Ame at the start of the street. Wander off into Yanaka's narrow back streets and it gets even better. You might stroll past the wooden house where Meiji-era novelist Natsume Soseki wrote his

masterpiece *I Am a Cat* or the house-turned-museum where painter Yokoyama Taikan lived. The pair were two of many artists, literati and bohemians who, in the main thanks to Yanaka's low rents, used to call the area home.

While Yanaka is best discovered by wandering aimlessly, letting the winding streets lead you where they will, make sure you find your way at some point to Yanaka Cemetery. The peaceful, incense-infused cemetery holds some 7,000 graves, including the resting place of the last shogun. It's also one of Tokyo's most tranquil spots except, that is, when the cherry blossoms turn much of its main walkways pink in early spring, attracting crowds of picnickers.

Opening Times Different shops along Yanaka Ginza close on different days. Most are open by 10.30 a.m. Yanaka Cemetery is open 24/7 (the office, where you can pick up a map of the famous graves, is open daily 8.30 a.m.–5.15 p.m.). **Getting There** Yanaka Ginza is a five-minute walk from the west exit of Nippori Station on the Yamanote Line. Yanaka Cemetery is one minute from the same station.

8 Akihabara
Japan's home electronics and geeky mecca

Akihabara, which is located almost halfway between the Imperial Palace area (page 26) and Ueno (page 33), has come to mean two things to the Japanese: electronics and *otaku*. The first of those associations can be traced back to the black market trading of radio components in the area, which began shortly after World War II and then morphed into the legitimate trading of home electronics and gadgetry that today has made Akihabara the home electronics retail center of Tokyo. The latter association is more recent, Akihabara becoming the focal point for *otaku* (which you can translate somewhere near to geek), initially on the back of video gaming in the late 1980s but more recently on *anime* (animation) and *manga* (comic books).

What that means for visitors to modern day Akihabara is that from side street computer component specialists to one-stop megastores like Yodobashi Akiba (page 36), you won't find a bigger or more varied collection of home electronics shops anywhere else in Japan. Nor will you see a better or at times more bizarre selection of stores specializing in *manga*,

anime, video games, cosplay (costume play) outfits and all manner of hobby goods and collectibles.

If you wanted to build your own robot, you'd come to Akiba—as Akihabara is often called—for parts. Want to collect models of every character ever to have appeared in a Godzilla movie? This is the place to find Mothra and more. Need to complete your poster collection of super cute (or super irritating, depending on your stance) teen idol girl group AKB48? Come here before seeking out a counselor. Or just come and have a browse, not only at the stores but of the occasional oddballs in fancy dress wandering the streets. You don't need to be an *otaku* or a techie to enjoy Akiba. For a fuller look at the area and a detailed run-down on many of its stores, look at the Akihabara and Shinjuku section on pages 36-7.

Opening Times Most shops in Akihabara open from 10 a.m. or 11 a.m. This might sound odd, but Akihabara is actually better on a weekend when it's busiest; you've got more chance to see some unusual sights then. **Getting There** Akihabara Station is on the JR Yamanote, Chuo-Sobu and Keihin-Tohoku lines and the Hibiya subway line.

9 Edo-Tokyo History Museum
Learn about Tokyo's fascinating and colorful past

Some Tokyophiles looking at this will be wondering how on earth the Edo-Tokyo Museum has been chosen ahead of the Tokyo National Museum (page 75) for this chapter. They have a point. The TNM in Ueno (page 33) has the largest and finest collection of Japanese artifacts anywhere in the world—some 100,000 pieces dating from the Jomon period to the early 20th century—but nowhere gives as much insight into the city of Tokyo and its development as the Edo-Tokyo museum.

Located in Ryogoku behind the country's main sumo stadium (page 80), the six-floor Edo-Tokyo History Museum is divided into several zones. There are special exhibition areas, cafés and off-limits storage areas on the lower floors, but it's the exhibits in the Edo Zone and Tokyo Zone on the fifth and sixth floors that mark the museum out for special attention. You enter the Edo Zone over a 25-meter (82-foot)-long wooden replica of the original Nihonbashi Bridge, the doorway to Edo for anyone traveling from places such as Kyoto or Nikko, and then proceed to take in incredibly detailed and evocative exhibits that include a full-scale replica of the kind of tenement houses in which Edo's lower classes lived and the decorative façade of a Kabuki playhouse.

The Western influences that helped transform the city and Japan's rapid modernization under the Meiji emperor are then brilliantly documented in the Tokyo Zone, as too are the devastating impacts of the Great Kanto Earthquake of 1923 and the air raids of World War II. There's a Model-A Ford from 1931, one of the foreign cars once used as taxis in Tokyo, which speaks of a time before Japan was producing its own automobiles. From the early Showa period (1930s), there's the part-original, part-replica house of the Yamagoya family, featuring a dining room and living room built in a European log house style but bedrooms built in a traditional Japanese style—a wonderful example of Japan on its first steps to modernization after centuries of feudal isolation.

Opening Times Tues–Sun 9.30 a.m.–5.30 p.m. (until 7.30 p.m. on Sat). **Getting There** A three-minute walk from the west exit of Ryogoku Station on the JR Sobu Line or one minute on foot from exit A4 of the Oedo subway line. **Contact** www.edo-tokyo-museum.or.jp **Admission Fee** ¥600.

10 Roppongi Hills and Tokyo Midtown
Two urban developments that have redefined Tokyo

Roppongi used to be the preserve of late night drinkers and restaurant-goers—just another drab piece of urban-ity by day that would come to life only after dark. Today, with two of the city's most fashionable urban redevelopments, it's become the epitome of cosmopolitan Tokyo.

The catalyst for change was billionaire Minoru Mori, head of the giant Mori Building Company, and the $2.5 billion Roppongi Hills complex he launched to much hype in 2003. With more than 200 shops, boutiques, restaurants, cafés and bars as well as the sleek Grand Hyatt Hotel, the stunning Mori Art Museum (page 76) located on the top floors of the complex's glistening main tower, plus, in separate buildings, the headquarters of Asahi TV and some of the city's most exclusive apartments, it was rightly billed as a "city within a city", breaking new ground for Tokyo with its scale and luxury. It set the stage for other sleek urban devel-opments that would soon follow nearby.

Not to be outdone by Mori, Mitsui Fudosan, Japan's largest real estate devel-oper, built a city within a city of its own—Tokyo Midtown—within shouting distance. Opened in 2007, Mitsui's complex is made up of five buildings and a central tower that, at 248 meters (814 feet) is the tallest building in Tokyo Prefecture. Its five-story Galleria is home to 73,000 square meters (790,000 square feet) of stores and restaurants, while the surrounding grounds include a spacious park and garden.

Where Roppongi Hills boasts the Grand Hyatt, Midtown has the five-star Ritz-Carlton (page 60), occupying the upper floors of its main tower. Midtown doesn't do badly for art either, with the 21_21 Design Sight gallery and workshop, created by renowned architect Tadao Ando and fashion designer Issey Miyake to showcase modern Japanese design, as well as the Suntory Museum of Art and its fine collection of traditional Japanese art.

The result is two cities within a city, standing face to face, combining to create the quintessential contemporary Tokyo experience.

Opening Times Varies by store, attraction and restaurant, but most places within Roppongi Hills and Midtown will be open by 11 a.m. Check the websites below. **Getting There** Roppongi Station is on the Hibiya and Oedo subway lines. **Contact** Roppongi Hills: www.roppongihills.com. Tokyo Midtown: www.tokyo-midtown.com.

11 A Visit to Oedo Hot Springs in Odaiba
A traditional bathhouse experience with a little Edo kitsch

I can think of no better Japanese tradition than getting naked with strangers for a long soak in steaming hot water. If you head out of the city, to places like Nikko (page 51) or Hakone (page 54), you'll have ample opportunity to try a hot spring bath. In Tokyo and other urban areas, it's an entirely different story. Thank the hot spring gods for Oedo Onsen Monogatori in Odaiba, Tokyo's largest artificial hot spring complex.

The baths at this *onsen* (hot spring bath) theme park include a classic *rotemburo* (outdoor bath) designed to feel as if you are soaking in a mountain rock pool as well as a lie-down massage bath and several other mineral-rich natural hot spring baths said to alleviate all manner of ailment, from stress to arthritis to dermatitis. Away from the main bathing area you can pop outside to the Japanese garden for a walk through its winding 50-meter (164-foot)-long foot bath, which in places is lined with pebbles and jagged rocks designed to massage your feet (admittedly, massage in this case at times means to inflict excruciating pain). If you have the stomach for it, you can follow that with a visit to the "Doctor Fish" foot bath (additional fee), where hundreds of tiny fish swarm over your feet to nibble away the dead skin.

Back inside, in an area designed to look like an Edo era town, there's a food court with a dozen or so small eateries. There are also several different spa treatments to try, a lounge with massage chairs and a sauna. For children there are traditional games to try and occasional street performances. You could easily spend all day here.

The only real challenge at Oedo Onsen is knowing what you are doing at times. Here are some quick tips. As you enter the lobby, take your shoes off and store them in one of the lockers off to your left, and then go to the reception desk where you'll be given an electronic wristband with which everything you buy inside will be scanned to your bill. At the next counter, pick up a colorful *yukata* robe to wear for the day (they have all sizes). Men and women split up here into separate changing rooms and then meet up again in the mock Edo town area after changing into their *yukata*. Like the changing rooms, the bathing areas (on the other side of the Edo area) are gender separated, too; as you approach the bathing zone, men are in the bathing rooms to the right, women to the left. As for the correct bathing etiquette, see page 86.

Opening Times Daily 11 a.m.–9 p.m. (last entry 7 p.m.). **Getting There** A several-minute walk from Telecom Center Station on the Yurikamome Line, which can be taken from Shimbashi (subway and JR lines). **Contact** www.ooedoonsen.jp/higaeri/english **Admission Fee** ¥2,480 weekdays, ¥2,680 weekends and public holidays (as of April 2014). Once inside, everything you eat, drink or buy will be charged to your bill, payable at reception upon leaving.

12 Shinjuku Gyoen Park
Tokyo's finest park is the perfect respite from the city

In spring, cherry blossoms briefly bathe Shinjuku Gyoen in a delicate pink hue. In summer, lush green foliage is punctuated by varicolored rose beds before autumn brings rich, earthy tones and fallen leaves carpet the sprawling lawns. On the few days of winter when snow falls on Tokyo, the park is quiet enough to hear the frost and snow crunch underfoot. Throughout the year, there really is no finer place to escape the rigors of the city without having to leave it.

Shinjuku's level of park perfection was a long time in the making. The park dates back to the Edo era when it was part of a *daimyo*'s residence, and it then became an imperial garden during the Meiji period before opening to the public shortly after World War II. Over those years it has developed into a wonderful mishmash of garden styles, its 57 hectares (140 acres) combining formal French garden designs, traditional Japanese elements, English landscaping and a greenhouse complex that is home to some 2,400 tropical and subtropical species. Encircling the lawns and ponds you can add to all that 20,000 trees, ranging from Himalayan cedars and bald cypresses to the blossoms that make the park's central lawn a stunning cherry blossom viewing spot in late March and early April.

What's just as amazing is the location. As you stroll in the peaceful grounds, silence threatened only by birdsong or the hum of summer cicadas, it's hard to believe you are within walking distance of the heaving streets of Shinjuku (page 37) and one of the world's busiest train stations. My advice for when Tokyo gets a little too busy for you is to pack up a picnic and a good book and take yourself off to Shinjuku Gyoen for a few hours.

Opening Times 9 a.m.–4.30 p.m. (last entry 4 p.m.). **Getting There** A 10-minute walk from JR Shinjuku Station (multiple lines) or a five-minute walk from either Shinjuku-gyoen-mae Station on the Marunouchi Line or Shinjuku 3-chome Station on the Toei Shinjuku Line. **Contact** www.env.go.jp/garden/shinjukugyoen **Admission Fee** ¥200.

13 A Hike Up Mount Takao
A taste of Japan's great outdoors on Tokyo's doorstep

With more than 70% of the country being mountainous, no matter where you go in Japan a good hike is never far away, even in Tokyo. Mount Takao (aka Takao-san) is a prime example. At 599 meters (1,965 feet), and with the option of taking a cable car or chairlift more than halfway to the summit, serious outdoor types wouldn't break a sweat on it, but it's proximity to central Tokyo and the opportunity it affords to take in a small part of Japan's stunning great outdoors make it a great day trip nonetheless.

In all, there are seven trails that lead to Takao-san's peak. While the most commonly used (by those who don't take the cable car, anyway) is trail #7, opt instead for the quieter trail #6, an at times steep route through forest that leads past streams and a waterfall, in the process revealing many of Takao's 500 or so types of wild flowers and plants. The reward for your effort—on a clear day, at least—will be majestic views from Takao-san's summit out west to Mount Fuji. On the way back down, take trail #1 so you can pass through the colorful 8th-century Yakuno-in Temple. In fact, for a very special experience related to the temple, visit Takao on the second Sunday in March for the Hiwatarisai fire ritual. Crowds flock to the event to watch *yamabushi* (monks who practice Shugendo Buddhism) walk barefoot over burning fires and smoldering coals, and many of the spectators end up gingerly doing the same after the coals have cooled to a safer temperature.

For information on longer hikes in the region, check out Lonely Planet's excellent *Hiking in Japan* guidebook or visit www.outdoorjapan.com.

Getting There The cable car and hiking trails are a five-minute walk from Takaosan-guchi Station on the Keio Line, which can be reached in about 50 minutes from Shinjuku. Allow up to two hours to hike from the station to the peak if you don't use the cable car. **Contact** www.takaotozan.co.jp. **Admission Fee** Free, but charges apply for the cable car or chairlift.

Rainbow Bridge connecting Odaiba with central Tokyo

Nijubashi Bridge over the Imperial Palace moat

Manga and *anime* advertisements in Akihabara

Gundam statue at Odaiba

Mount Fuji looming over Lake Ashi in Hakone

CHAPTER 2
EXPLORING TOKYO

Nezu Shrine

At turns futuristic, at others unerringly traditional, in places tranquil but most often invigoratingly un-Zen like, the patchwork of districts that comprise Tokyo's core make the city hard to define. Next to the chic stores and fashions of Omotesando are the sanctity of Meiji Jingu Shrine and the brash teen fashions of Takeshita-dori. Rubbing shoulders with the traditional landscaping of Hama-Rikyu Gardens are the glistening towers of the Shidome area and the sprawling warehouses of the Tsukiji Fish Market. Like a mini Tokyo within Tokyo, Shinjuku has bits of everything. The area guides that follow will help you discover not just the best Tokyo has to offer but each of the contrasts, faces, traditions and quirks that make the city such a vibrant and unforgettable place to visit.

EXPLORING TSUKIJI, GINZA AND THE IMPERIAL PALACE
A tour of downtown Tokyo

See pull-out map H7; H10; J9–10

Some cities, it is said, never sleep but Tokyo isn't one of them. Despite the crushing crowds of the morning rush-hour trains as millions of office workers descend on central Tokyo to meet their 9 a.m. check-in, Tokyo doesn't have all that much for early risers. Besides temples and shrines, most tourist attractions and shops don't open until about 10 a.m. The **Tsukiji Fish Market** is a welcome exception to that rule.

By 5.30 a.m., just as the first trains of the day are starting up their engines, Tsukiji is already at fever pitch, its frenetic auctions and army of 60,000 wholesalers, buyers and shippers combining to shift somewhere in the region of 2,000 tons of seafood and other fresh produce daily. A visit here for the early morning tuna auctions is well worth a pre-dawn alarm call (see Tokyo's 'Don't Miss' Sights, page 11,

for a more detailed look at both the auctions and Tsukiji Market in general), but even if you get here by 9 a.m., several hours after the auctions have ended, you'll still be able to soak up Tsukiji's bustling atmosphere and land a great *sushi* breakfast at one of the many small *sushi* restaurants in and around the outer market area.

By the time you finish breakfast, Tsukiji's neighbors will just about be waking up—and there are several good areas nearby to check out. Ten minutes southwest are **Hama-Rikyu Gardens** (Tokyo's Best Parks and Gardens, page 77), a lovely mix of landscaped stroll garden and less-tended flower fields, above which the gleaming skyscrapers of the Shiodome district loom large. Heading a similar distance north from Tsukiji, taking Shin-ohashi-dori and then turning left onto Harumi-dori, comes the **Kabuki-za Theater**, Tokyo's premier venue for Kabuki—a classical dance-drama defined by its elaborate costumes and make-up and the heavily stylized approach taken by the players. Reopened in 2013 after a long period of refurbishment, but still with a very traditional design, it's at least worth passing by to take in the building itself, if not to book tickets for one of the plays (www.kabuki-za.co.jp; English audio guides are

Chuo-dori in Ginza is home to numerous high-end brands

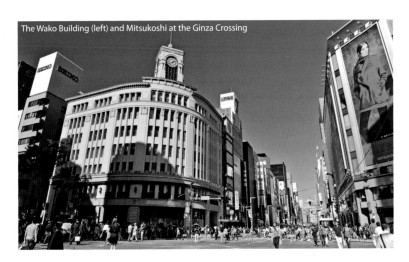
The Wako Building (left) and Mitsukoshi at the Ginza Crossing

available, and you can also attend for a single act rather than sitting through a full performance of several hours).

From Kabuki-za, it's a walk of several hundred meters farther up the road to the **Ginza Crossing**, the center point of the **Ginza** area—Tsukiji's most illustrious neighbor. Ask any Japanese about Ginza and you can guarantee one of the first things they will tell you is that the area is home to many of Tokyo's finest restaurants, or many of the city's most exclusive department stores and boutiques, or even its most expensive hostess clubs. Whichever response you get, it'll somehow tie into wealth and the conspicuous consumption of it.

That association with wealth goes back centuries, to 1612 when Tokugawa Ieyasu chose Ginza as the site for a silver coin mint (*gin za* actually means silver mint), but it wasn't really until the onset of the Meiji era, 260 years later, that Ginza began to take its current shape. From the late 1870s onwards, after centuries of Edo isolation, the Western-influenced Meiji government took to rebuilding Ginza and other central districts, replacing the cramped wood-built neighborhoods,

which were susceptible to fast-spreading fire, with European-style architecture and street planning. Rickshaws gave way to horse-drawn trams and later electric trams, while new paved sidewalks and street gaslights blended with brick and stone buildings (designed and built by European architectures and later their Japanese apprentices) to give Ginza a very Western make-over.

At Ginza Crossing you'll see one of the few remaining buildings from that Meiji-era transformation. Originally built in 1894 and then reconstructed after the Great Kanto Earthquake of 1923, the curved granite façade and clock tower of the **Wako Building** is one of Tokyo's last-standing pre-war structures. Inside is the prestigious department store Wako (www.wako.co.jp), founded under a different name by the creator of Seiko watches in 1881. Across the road from Wako (on your right, if you've just walked from Kabuki-za) **Mitsukoshi** department store, guarded at its entrance by a bronze lion that looks to have come from the same pride as those at Nelson's Column in London, is another of the high-end department stores that have helped to

The Imperial Palace's Fushimi Yagura tower and Nijubashi Bridge

build Ginza's long-held reputation as Tokyo's premier shopping district (although Omotesando, page 27, might have something to say about that). Turn right here and walk down Chuo-dori and there's also a plush **Matsuya** department store along with the architecturally striking flagship stores of several European boutiques—**Chanel**, in a 10-story building with 70,000 light-emitting diodes creating a changeable façade being the most impressive on the eyes, although the **Cartier**, **Bulgari** and **Mikomoto** buildings nearby come fairly close. The brand names extend into the arteries leading off of Chuo-dori and Harumi-dori, where they share the streets with cafés, bistros and restaurants as well as more affordable Japanese and international high-street fashion brands like **Gap**, **Uniqlo**, **Muji**, **Zara** and **H&M**.

Leaving Ginza behind, there's one other thing that can't be overlooked in the area—the **Imperial Palace** (www.kunaicho.go.jp; also see page 79 for the palace jogging route), which is a 10-15 minute walk northwest from the Ginza Crossing along Harumi-dori. Home to the imperial family, the palace and the majority of its 109-hectare (270-acre) grounds are off-limits but that that doesn't stop busloads of tourists visiting the outer grounds year round to get a glimpse of the palace's iconic Fushimi Yagura tower protruding through dense woods—the stone double arches of Nijubashi Bridge dominating the foreground as it straddles the moat protecting the inner palace—before heading to the palace's pleasant **East Gardens** (www.kunaicho.go.jp) to take in the traditional (albeit not Tokyo's most noteworthy) garden landscaping.

Time Required A full day. **Getting There** Start at Tsukiji Fish Market, which is a one-minute walk from either Tsukiji Station (exit 1 or 2) on the Hibiya Line or Tsukiji-shijo Station (exit A1) on the Oedo Line. If you go for the tuna auctions, you'll need to take a taxi as the trains won't be running that early. To leave the Ginza area at the end of the day, you can take the Marunouchi Line, Ginza Line or Hibiya Line. **Where to Eat** Ginza's department stores all have restaurants on their upper floors, many of which offer decent lunches from around ¥1,000. For something with atmosphere, you could also stop for lunch (or dinner) for *yakitori* (grilled chicken) at one of the small restaurants spilling out onto the street under the elevated railway track that runs between Shimbashi and Yurakucho stations. You'll walk under here on the way from Ginza to the Imperial Palace—just turn left and you'll soon see the *yakitori* joints. For dinner, Ginza teems with high-end options (see the listing website www.timeout.jp for some ideas), but instead you could opt for a traditional *izakaya* in Yurakucho with a trip to Shin Hinomoto (page 68). **Insider Tip** Head to the colorful basement-level food floor of Mitsukoshi department store where you can often pick up small free samples from the deli counters—a great way to sample some interesting local flavors.

EXPLORING OMOTESANDO, HARAJUKU AND SHIBUYA
Haute couture meets tradition and youthful street fashion

See pull-out map C8–D10

Omotesando-dori is a great example of how Tokyo frequently manages to reinvent itself. Although the 800-meter (2,625-foot) stretch of zelkova-lined boulevard was originally shaped in the Taisho era (1912–26) to form the approach to **Meiji Jingu Shrine** (Tokyo's 'Don't Miss' Sights, page 9), it has since become anything but a solemn procession. **Omotesando-dori** is now Japan's most chic and arguably most prestigious high-end shopping street, not to mention a showcase for some of Tokyo's most interesting modern architecture.

The street's modern-day image has come from being home to glitzy stores like **Louis Vuitton**, **Prada**, **Armani**,

Burberry, **Gucci**, **Paul Stuart**, **Dior** and many others of that ilk, as well as Tadao Ando's architecturally impressive **Omotesando Hills** mall (see Tokyo's 'Don't Miss' Sights, page 10, for more on that and other stand-out structures along Omotesando-dori), yet once you leave Omotesando's main drag behind and delve into the side streets that snake off of it, things change quickly. After walking along most of Omotesando-dori (starting at exit B4 of Omotesnado Station), stroll along **Ura-Harajuku** (aka Cat Street), which cuts across Omotesando-dori just after the northern end of Omotesando Hills, and the international heavyweights give way to cafés, the small fashion boutiques of young local designers, and even the occasional thrift store. If you were to choose any place in Tokyo to stop and get a handle on the latest street fashions, the arteries of Omotesando would be the place to do it.

Back on Omotesando-dori the road continues up to the **Harajuku Crossing**, where the youthfulness of Ura-Harajuku continues. Straight on from here are branches of **Lacoste** and then **Zara**

The brand name-lined Omotesando-dori

Takeshita-dori in Harajuku

and beauty stores catering to young women, while beyond are branches of **H&M** and **Forever 21**. Another minute on from there is the start of Harajuku's most well-known street, **Takeshita-dori** (page 29), a long, narrow stretch of road that leads toward Harajuku Station. If you are in a hurry for a train, go a different way; fighting through the crowds of teenage shoppers who come here to check out the cosplay, goth and quirky fashion stores requires either some kind of shopping lust or a combination of whiskey and aspirin.

before the street reaches Harajuku Station and the entrance to Meiji Jingu Shrine. Look left instead at the Harajuku Crossing and there are branches of **Levi's**, **UT Store** (which sells affordable and fun designer T-shirts) and the landmark **Condomania**—no prizes for guessing what this tiny store specializes in. Look right and you get the **La Foret Harajuku** department store (www.laforet.ne.jp/en), home to more than 100 fashion, accessory

Fortunately, there is respite from all that, if you need it. Once you are at **Harajuku Station** another transformation takes place if you cross the bridge over the train lines—around which at weekends you'll often seen teenage cosplayers dressed as blood-soaked nurses, Little Bo Peep clones and the like—and head into **Meiji Jingu Shrine**. Built in the 1910s to enshrine the souls of the Emperor Meiji and his consort, the Empress Shoken, the

Arty Options: Omotesando's Galleries and Museums

For a break from the crowds, check out some of Harajuku and Omotesando's line-up of **galleries and museums**. The **La Foret Museum** on the sixth floor of La Foret Harajuku (see above) holds a varied mix of art exhibitions and events, while in the back streets just behind it the **Ota Memorial Museum of Art** (www.ukiyo-ota-muse.jp) houses a fantastic collection of 12,000 *ukiyo-e* (woodblock prints). Not far from there, heading south into the streets across from the bottom end of Takeshita-dori, comes the **Design Festa Gallery**, one of the best places in Tokyo to check out freestyle art, be that abstract painting, video installations, photography or anything in between on show in its dozens of small exhibition spaces. And in very stark contrast to that is the **Nezu Museum** (www.

nezu-muse.or.jp), a short walk away from the Omotesando Station end of Omotesando-dori, where a fine collection of more than 7,000 pre-modern Japanese and other Asian arts is housed in a stunning building by architect Kuma Kengo that combines sleek modern design with traditional Japanese sensibilities.

Design Festa Gallery

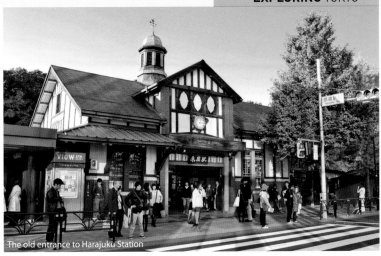
The old entrance to Harajuku Station

shrine (see page 9) provides a tranquil and spacious contrast to the crowds and chaos of Takeshita-dori. Its inner precinct (the Naien) is enshrouded by 28 hectares (70 acres) of towering forest which also surrounds an iris garden that blooms into life in June, while the 32-hectare (80-acre) outer precinct (the Gaien) mixes parkland (see Yoyogi Park, page 78) with sporting and leisure facilities that are a legacy of the 1964 Tokyo Olympics.

After Harajuku, delve deeper into youthful Tokyo by catching the Yamanote Line one stop to **Shibuya**. Before cell phones became the most ubiquitous item in Tokyo, finding someone at Shibuya's most popular meeting point was like locating a needle in a 1,000-man rugby scrum. The landmark, a statue of a dog called Hachiko who, in the 1920s and 1930s would come to Shibuya Station every afternoon to welcome his master home from work and continued doing so even after his master's death (a story of loyalty that particularly resonates with the Japanese), seems perpetually surrounded by teens and twenty somethings about to go shopping, drinking or dancing—as they move on their numbers continually being replenished by the crowds flowing

out of Shibuya Station or descending upon Hachiko from the Shibuya Crossing.

As with Harajuku, you don't come to Shibuya for a spot of peace and quiet. By day, the crowds that flock here come mainly to shop. Many of the fashionable young men and women you'll see coming out of the station and heading over the Shibuya Crossing—some in fashions and accessories that teeter precariously on the boundary between colorful and gar-ish, occasionally tumbling spectacularly onto the garish side—will be heading to places like the **Shibuya 109** building (page 71), an eight-floor collection of more than 100 small fashion boutiques. Others will be bound for the nearby **Center Gai** shopping precinct, home to a multitude of fashion stores and, in a similar vein to Takeshita-dori (page 28) or Ura-Harajuku (page 27), a good place to get a first glimpse of the latest teen and street fashions before they explode across other parts of Japan.

Not that the shopping in Shibuya is all teen and twenty something-centered. Koen-dori, which runs toward Yoyogi Park, is home to major department stores such as **Marui** (www.0101.co.jp), **Seibu** (www2.seibu.jp) and **Parco** (http://

Shibuya Crossing, Tokyo's most crowded intersection where shoulder bumps are guaranteed

shibuya.parco.jp), while looming large over the east side of Shibuya Station is one of Tokyo's latest major urban complexes—**Shibuya Hikarie** (www.hikarie.jp). Opened in 2012 and hoping to entice an older and deeper pocketed shopper than Shibuya's norm, the 34-story multipurpose tower combines office spaces, cafés, restaurants, art spaces, theaters and lots of slickly designed shops selling international designer fashions and interiors goods. Another broad interest shopping option is the head branch of **Tokyu** department store (www.tokyu-dept.co.jp/honten), which houses a similar mix of fashion, food and interiors, along with a neighboring "culture village" (Tokyu Bunkamura; www.bunkamura.co.jp) that contains cinemas, major concert halls and an art museum.

Come nightfall, however, and Shibuya is still very much for a younger crowd, be that in its bars and *izakaya* (pubs-cum-restaurants) or in its line-up of clubs, which between them cover everything from rock to techno and include top venues like Club Quattro, Dommune, Liquid Room and Womb (see pages 67–9). For up-to-date information on the best bars and clubs in the area (and in Omotesando and Harajuku), check out the listings at Metropolis magazine (http://metropolis.co.jp) or Time Out Tokyo (www.timeout.jp).

Time Required A full day, best starting after 10 a.m. or 11 a.m. once the stores on Omotesando have opened. **Getting There** Omotesando-dori can be accessed at one end by Omotesando Station on the Chiyoda, Ginza and Hanzomon subway lines, and the other by Meiji Jingumae Station on the Chiyoda Line and Harajuku Station on the JR Yamanote Line. The best place to start this day out is from exit B4 of Omotesando Station, which brings you out on the far end of the tree-lined Omotesando-dori. From Harajuku to Shibuya, it's easiest to take the Yamanote Line (one stop) and then come out of Shibuya Station at the Hachiko exit. When leaving Shibuya, you can use the JR Yamanote Line, the Ginza, Hanzomon and Fukutoshin subways lines, the Toyoko Line or the Keio Inokashira Line. **Where to Eat** There are plenty of great restaurants, cafés and bistros in the side streets shooting off of Omotesando (check out www.timeout.jp for the most up-to-date listings), and Omotesando Hills is another good place to stop for lunch, with more than a dozen sleek cafés and restaurants there. Alternatively, on a weekend visit, pop into the UNU Farmer's Market (Tokyo's Best Shopping, page 72), a short walk from Omotesando Station away from Omotesando-dori. Later in the day, for places to drink or party in Shibuya, check out the Nightlife section on page 67.

EXPLORING ASAKUSA
The heart of Tokyo's Original "Low City"

See pull-out map L4; M4

Asakusa, situated next to the Sumida River in Tokyo's northeast, is where the *shitamachi* (see box, page 32) heart beats the loudest. For around a hundred years prior to World War II, the area was Tokyo's premier entertainment district, teeming with bars, *izakaya* and eateries, and a hub for theaters of all kinds, from vaudeville houses and striptease joints to venues for classical performing arts. In the thousand years or so before then, however, things were very different. Asakusa had steadily grown up around **Senso-ji Temple** (Tokyo's 'Don't Miss' Sights, page 13), which after being founded in the early 600s to house a statue of Kannon supposedly found by two brothers fishing in the Sumida River, prospered in the Edo era as the tutelary temple of the ruling Tokugawas.

Senso-ji, a two-minute walk from Asakusa subway station, is still Asakusa's focal point (and the best place to start exploring the area), the temple's giant halls and gateways holding back the encircling urban sprawl of eastern Tokyo to create an enclave of tradition. Not that it shares the calm and serenity that many of Japan's most venerable temples and shrines exude. With the stalls that surround it and a steady flow of visitors year round—tourists and locals alike—the temple complex is always lively, but especially so along **Nakamise-dori**, the colorful stall-lined street that leads from Senso-ji's main gateway, the towering Kaminari-mon, through to its five-story pagoda and main temple hall. Away from the temple, the rest of Asakusa can be just as energetic. In May, the **Sanja Matsuri** (page 82), a festival in honor of Senso-ji's founders that sees the streets of Asakusa taken over by a frenetic procession of portable shrines, attracts close to two million onlookers. Along with Tokyo's biggest fireworks display, the **Sumidagawa Hanabi Taikai**, in July (Tokyo's Best Events and Festivals, page 81), and a sweat-drenched **Samba festival** (www.asakusa-samba.jp) in August, it's one of several times each year when Asakusa explodes into life.

The pagoda and Hozomon gateway at Senso-ji Temple

Shitamachi: The Low City

Some call *shitamachi* the part of Edo (later called Tokyo) where "the common people" lived. Others liken it to east-end London, its residents the Japanese equivalent of Cockneys. Both of those are fair descriptions, but the fact that the *shita* and *machi* parts of the term are often translated directly into English as "downtown" or "low city" can throw up some misunderstandings. *Shitamachi* is very different to the English use of downtown as a central district, and "low" has nothing to do with the class of the area's residents. The term actually originates from the level of the land in the area. In Edo, the land to the southeast of what is now the Imperial Palace (then it was the site of Edo Castle) was lowland, while the land to the northwest was a plateau. As the city developed under Tokugawa rule, this lowland area developed into the (often cramped) home of artisans, merchants and laborers, and a rich working-class culture that still defines the *shitamachi* developed.

Several minutes' walk west of Senso-ji's pagoda, heading left when facing the steps of the main hall, is a remnant from Asakusa's entertainment days, the retro **Hanayashiki Amusement Park** (Tokyo's Best Kid-friendly Attractions, page 74). Home to Japan's oldest and arguably least terrifying roller coaster as well as many other vintage attractions, the park might not be the perfect fit for kids weaned on PlayStation and Disneyland, but young children will love it. Just southwest of the park comes the northern end of **Rokku Broadway**, a street known for theaters such as **Engei Hall** (www.asakusaengei.com), which puts on a daily bill of slapstick comedy shows and traditional comic storytelling. The acts are all performed in Japanese but the humor is often so visual that it transcends language barriers—and even if it doesn't, watching the audience howl, holler and heckle is entertainment of itself.

Walk ten minutes east of the theaters and Asakusa's merchant roots are soon recalled on the still-thriving **Kappabashi-dori** (Tokyo's Best Shopping, page 72), where there are some 200 stores specializing in different items for the restaurant trade, from shop-front lanterns and

plastic replicas of food for window displays to places where you can buy disposable chopsticks in bulk. From there, if you are in the mood for a very long day out, you could even continue walking on to **Ueno and Yanesen** (page 33), which are covered in the next section, or instead lengthen the day by combining Asakusa with the **Tokyo Skytree** (page 12; also below). Another option is to head back to Asakusa and hop on a **river boat cruise** (page 14) down the Sumida River.

Time Required A half-day is enough to take in Asakusa and Kappabashi-dori but allow a full day if you add a trip to the nearby Tokyo Skytree. **Getting There** Asakusa Station is on the Ginza Line, Toei Asakusa Line and Tobu Isesaki Line. Senso-ji is a several-minute, well-signposted walk from the station and from there you can easily cover all the main sights on foot. **Where to Eat** For lunch or dinner in Asakusa, you can soak up the *shitamachi* vibe best at either one of the *yakitori* (grilled chicken) joints that spill out onto the streets south of Engei Hall or stop for *izakaya* fare and a fiery cocktail of spirits called Denki Bran (electric brandy) along with the locals at **Kamiya Bar**. **Insider Tip** Combine Asakusa with a morning or evening trip up the **Tokyo Skytree** (Tokyo's 'Don't Miss' Sights, page 12), a 15-minute walk east of Asakusa on the other side of the Sumida River. You'll need both a head for heights and a spare few thousand yen to look down upon Tokyo from the Skytree's glass-bottomed observation decks.

EXPLORING
UENO AND YANESEN
A day exploring "old Tokyo"

See pull-out map J2-3; K3-4

Like Asakusa, the **Ueno** district has never strayed too far from its *shitamachi* roots. To understand that, you need look no further than the lively **Ameya Yokocho street market** across the road from Ueno Station's main exit, which first flourished on the back of black market trading as Tokyo dusted off the ashes of World War II and began its remarkable recovery and growth.

The focus of the vocal touts and vendors here is purely on legitimate goods nowadays (OK, you might find the occasional knock-off fashion brand)—fish, vegetables, dried foods and teas, and low-price clothing and bags making up the bulk of the stores. Although Ameya Yokocho (familiarly known as Ameyoko)

is technically a single narrow street packed with small shops and crowds and overlooked by the elevated JR rail tracks, the other streets running parallel with it and leading on from its far end are packed with just as many stalls, not to mention budget eateries, *izakaya* and the occasional *tachinomiya* (standing-only bar). Nowhere else in Ueno is as bustling or as *shitamachi* as this.

A few minutes' walk west from Ameyoko, **Ueno Park** provides a very different atmosphere. Spread over 54 hectares (133 acres), the park was one of Japan's first public parks when established in the 1870s on what was once temple grounds. There are still historic religious buildings within the park, most notably a **Tosho-gu shrine** and **a five-story pagoda** built in the 1600s for shogun Tokugawa Ieyasu. The park is also home to several large **lily-covered ponds** around which food vendors set up at weekends, a small **boating lake**, Tokyo's biggest zoo, **Ueno Zoo** (www. tokyo-zoo.net/zoo/ueno), cherry blossom trees that turn many of its walkways a delicate pink in spring, and some of the city's most interesting museums. In fact,

Ameya Yokocho street market in Ueno

Cherry blossom season in Ueno Park

with the **Shitamachi Museum** (www.taitocity.net/taito/shitamachi), **Tokyo Metropolitan Art Museum** (www.tobikan.jp), **National Museum of Nature and Science** (www.kahaku.go.jp), **University Art Museum** (www.geidai.ac.jp/museum), **National Museum of Western Art** (www.nmwa.go.jp) and **Tokyo National Museum** (www.tnm.jp), nowhere else in Tokyo comes close to matching Ueno for the concentration and quality of its museums.

Should the urge take you, you could visit all the museums in one very long day out but, if not, at least try seeing the Shitamachi History Museum at the southern end of the park. From the outside you'll struggle to find a drabber museum but inside it brings the history of Tokyo's *shitamachi* (page 32) areas to life with exhibits that include a reconstruction of a 1920s tenement row. After that, move to the northern end of the park for the magnificent Tokyo National Museum (page 75). With more than 100,000 artifacts dating as far back as 3000 BC, it has the biggest and best collection of Japanese history in the world.

From the northwestern end of Ueno Park you are a short walk away from one of Tokyo's most atmospheric old areas, the winding, narrow streets of **Yanaka**, one of three adjoining neighborhoods (along with Nezu and Sendagi) that have come to be collectively called Yanesen. Having escaped the worst of the wartime bombing and the damage from the 1923 Great Kanto Earthquake, and also having managed to avoid the neon-fronted pachinko parlors, characterless restaurant chains and giant supermarkets that now blight many of Tokyo's residential neighborhoods, there is nowhere better for getting a taste of old Tokyo.

Yanaka Ginza, the Yanaka area's main shopping street, which is home to mom-and-pop stores and traditional craft shops, is covered in more detail along with **Yanaka Cemetery** on page 15 (Tokyo's 'Don't Miss' Sights), so we will skip that here and jump ahead into the maze of back streets that shoot off of Yanaka Ginza. Walking the alleyways of Yanaka takes you past dozens of small temples. Some are tucked next to old wooden houses, others near small craft workshops or beside rice shops, tofu makers, greengrocers and other specialist stores that have long been lost to supermarkets in other parts of Tokyo. Looking at it, it's not hard to understand why over the years Yanesen has also acquired a bit of a bohemian reputation.

Novelist Natsume Soseki (author of *I am a Cat*, *Botchan* and *Kokoro*) lived in Yanaka for a while in the Meiji era, while sculptor Asakura Fumio built a house near the Yanaka Cemetery's northern end in the mid-1930s. Today, the three-story building, which combines traditional Japanese architecture and landscape gardening with modernist influences, is open to the public as the worthwhile **Asakura Choso Museum** (www.taito-city.net/taito/asakura/english). The traditional elements that define Yanesen are still punctuated by the artsy. Occasionally you'll find a hip café in one of Yanesen's old wooden buildings, while contemporary art galleries such as the wonderful **Scai the Bathhouse** (www.scaithebathhouse.com/en), which is built in a renovated public bathhouse by the southern end of the cemetery, and **Space Oguraya** (www.oguraya.gr.jp), still give Yanesen strong artistic credentials.

Leaving that behind, Nezu's main contribution to Yanesen is the most striking and important of the area's religious structures, **Nezu Jinja** (www.nedujinja.or.jp). This shrine was supposedly founded 1,900 years ago in nearby Sendagi by the priest Yamato Takero no Mikoto but was rebuilt in Nezu by the fifth Tokugawa shogun, Tsunayoshi, in the early 1700s. Remarkably for a city that has been devastated on several occasions since then, the original Gongen-style structures are still there, all designated as nationally Important Cultural Properties. The azalea festival here in April and May, when 3,000 azaleas come into bloom around

The *torii*-covered pathway at Nezu Shrine

the dozens of red *torii* gateways that cover parts of the shrine's pathways, is an annual highlight, but a visit here any time of year is more than worth the walk.

Time Required A full day although you could choose to explore just Ueno or just Yanesen if you only have half a day available. **Getting There** Ueno Station is on the Yamanote Line and several other JR lines as well as the Hibiya and Ginza subway lines. The Keisei Line also stops in Ueno, at Keisei-Ueno Station. If you wanted to visit only Yanesen, start at Yanaka Ginza, which is a five-minute walk from the west exit of Nippori Station on the Yamanote Line. Yanaka Cemetery is one minute from the west exit of the same station. If you finish the day with Nezu Shrine, you can take the Chiyoda subway line at either Nezu or Sendagi stations. **Where to Eat** The streets parallel to and leading off of Ameyoko are home to many small eateries good for lunch or dinner, not to mention watering holes for the evening. Ueno Station also has some restaurants connected to it, including branches of familiar coffee chains and a Hard Rock Café (if you crave something other than Japanese food!). **Insider Tip** Museum hoppers might want to get a Grutt Pass. This ticket booklet allows one-time access or discounted admission to 77 facilities in and around Tokyo, including all of Ueno's museums, for just ¥2,000. The Grutt Pass can be bought at any of those facilities as well as at Tourist Information offices. It's valid for two months from the first day of use. See www.rekibun.or.jp/grutto/index.html for details. When planning a visit, be aware that many museums close on Mondays.

EXPLORING
AKIHABARA AND SHINJUKU
From home electronics center to melting pot

See pull-out map C6; D5–7; K5

Akihabara, as you'll see in the section on Tokyo's Best Shopping (page 71), is famous in Japan for home electronics and geekiness. It doesn't take long to see why when you visit. As soon as you step out of Akihabara Station, you are met with giant home electronics department stores such as **Laox, Yodobashi, Akky** and **Ishimaru Denki**. The biggest and best of the major players here, **Yodobashi Akiba** (page 71), opened on the east side of the station in 2005 and features six floors of home electronics covering everything from the latest cameras and cell phones to computers and massage chairs. Filling the niches

ignored by the big stores, Akihabara is also home to hundreds of smaller specialist retailers, places like **Thanko** (www. thanko.jp), specializing in quirky electronics that include odd-shaped USB devices and Bond-esque binoculars with built-in video recorder, and **Tsukumo Robot Kingdom** (http://robot.tsukumo. co.jp), which focuses on all sorts of robots, robot parts and kits.

Then, of course, comes the geeky (*otaku*) side. Although *otaku* have a socially awkward, nerdy image, their impact on Akiba (as Akihabara is familiarly known) and Japan's economy has been nothing short of miraculous; Akihabara is now firmly positioned at the centre of an *otaku* consumer market estimated to be worth more than 400 billion yen annually. Wander through the plethora of comic stores, costume shops and video game stores that compete for space with the electronics on and around Akiba's main street, Chuo-dori, and you'll see every *otaku* taste catered for, from overly cute *anime* characters to bizarre erotic *manga*. In particular, the large

Akihabara's main street

Donkihote (named, strangely, after Don Quixote; www.donki.com) has an entire floor dedicated to *anime* and *manga* costumes, while the small **Tokyo Anime Center** (www.animecenter.jp) on the fourth floor of **Akihabara UDX Building** has information on the latest happenings in Japanese animation and is home to a 3D theater and recording studio, as well as hosting numerous events. Another stand-out is **Mandrake** (www.mandarake.co.jp/en/shop/cmp.html) in the back streets on the opposite side of Chuo-dori to Donkihote, which has eight floors dedicated to comics and collectibles related to everything from Godzilla to Ultraman. Then there are stores like **Gee Store Akiba**, a minute up the main street from Donkihote and then across the road, which specializes solely in cosplay outfits and related goods.

Not that this part of the city is only about electrical goods and geeks. A few hundred meters west of Akihabara's main shopping street is the **Kanda Myojin** shrine, which was in place centuries before any *anime*-obsessed teens. Said to have been founded in the 730s in the Otemachi area near the current Imperial Palace and then relocated to its present location in 1616 by the first shogun Tokugawa Ieyasu, partly so he could use the former site to build better defenses for Edo Castle and partly because it enshrined Taira-no-Masakado, a popular anti-authority figure in the 900s, whose posthumous influence Tokugawa didn't want affecting his rule. The shrine's main claim to fame is its centuries-old festival, the **Kanda Matsuri**, one of the country's largest traditional events. Held annually on the weekend closest to May 15, but only on a major scale in years ending in odd numbers, the major version of the *matsuri* features processions of men in Edo-era costumes, portable shrines and

Akihabara's stores sell everything from *anime* to electronics

priests on horseback. About the only thing that comes close to being as spectacular on the eye are the *anime*-loving cosplayers you'll probably see on any normal visit to Akihabara.

The Akihabara area can be done as a stand-alone trip over several hours, but with a fairly quick train ride you could also combine it with a few hours in **Shinjuku** to make a full day out and about (from Akihabara Station you can get to Shinjuku on the JR Chuo Line). From its high-rise business district to the red lights of Kabuki-cho, the bohemian bars of Golden Gai, its shops and its magnificent park, nowhere else in Tokyo is as varied as Shinjuku. More often than not Shinjuku is brash, crowded and neon lit, but it still has pockets of tradition and down-to-earth side streets that ooze an old urban atmosphere that the march toward modernization has typically cast aside in Tokyo. Unlike the cosmopolitan Roppongi or Omotesando, Shinjuku is the modern part of Tokyo that has no great allusions of being Western.

A trip to Shinjuku starts with one of the busiest train stations in the world. If you hate crowds, hold tight! More than 3.5 million people pass through the 36 platforms and 200 exits of **Shinjuku Station** daily, making it one of the easiest

Shinjuku at night, with Mount Fuji in the distance

places in Tokyo to get hopelessly lost and bewildered. You might not have much choice in where you start exploring Shinjuku, but if you can, find the signs for the west exit and work your way gently into Shinjuku with the relatively calm west side, home to the area's high-rise business district and skyscrapers that house hotels like the **Park Hyatt** (see page 61 for that and page 68 for its bar and restaurant) as well as the towering Kenzo Tange-designed **Tokyo Metropolitan Government Building** (www. metro.tokyo.jp), whose twin 45-story towers have free **observation decks** from where you can take in tremendous views of Mount Fuji to the west and sprawling cityscapes in all directions. The west side also has a collection of major **home electronics stores**, similar to those in Akihabara (page 36), as well as several camera shops, such as MAP Camera (page 71), which is a great place to pick up pristine used gear.

Head to the other side of Shinjuku Station and things get more crowded and hectic. Here you'll get access to Shinjuku's main shopping areas and, along with branches of affordable fashion stores like **Muji**, **Uniqlo** and **Zara**, major **department stores** such as **Takashimaya**, **Marui** and the venerable **Isetan**. And yet, from there you'll also not be far from a moment or two of calm at **Shinjuku Gyoen**, a candidate for being Tokyo's finest garden (Tokyo's 'Don't Miss' Sights, page 20). The park's blend of formal French garden designs, traditional Japanese elements and English landscaping are wonderful year round, but in the spring, when cherry blossoms briefly bathe the park in a lovely soft pink, there is nowhere better in the city.

Come evening, after the gates to Shinjuku Gyoen are locked for the night and as the office workers in the west-side towers are beginning to leave their desks, east Shinjuku really comes into its own. In stark contrast to the peace and quiet of its park, Shinjuku is home to Japan's most notorious red-light district, **Kabuki-cho**, a five-minute walk from the station's

The entrance to Kabuki-cho, Tokyo's main red-light district, but also a good hunting ground for restaurants and bars

east exit. In truth, while Kabuki-cho is the realm of numerous shady sex clubs and *yakuza*-owned establishments, there are also plenty of great legitimate bars, restaurants and small music venues among the area's 4,000 or so establishments, which spill over into the neighboring area of **Shin Okubo** to the north (known as "Little Asia" because of its profusion of Korean and Southeast Asian stores and restaurants) and, directly east, **Golden Gai**, a maze of narrow lanes crammed with tiny bars that have traditionally attracted a bohemian blend of artists, writers and other "creatives". If you want to finish your day of exploring with a drink, you'll be hard pressed to find a better place to go bar hunting. Just be aware that many of the bars in Golden Gai can have seating charges upwards of ¥1,000 and often turn away non-regulars. Try the baroque-looking **Albatross G** (www.alba-s.com), the 1960s and 1970s rock, blues and soul den **Happy** (no website), **Asyl** (http://asyl.exblog.jp/), which is owned by a

world music nut, or the hospital-themed (you read that right) **Tachibana Shinsatsushitsu** (no website).

Time Required A full day starting after 10 a.m. once the stores begin to open. For more information on other stores and the latest trends in Akihabara, check out the excellent www.dannychoo.com.
Getting There Start the day at Akihabara Station, which is served by the JR Yamanote, Chuo-Sobu and Keihin-Tohoku lines as well as the Hibiya subway line and the Tsukuba Express (the latter of which isn't of much use for reaching other parts of Tokyo as it heads east into Chiba and Ibaraki prefectures). From Akihabara Station the easiest way to get to Shinjuku is with the JR Chuo Line (18 mins). When leaving Shinjuku, you'll have several options as Shinjuku Station acts as a hub between central Tokyo and Tokyo's western suburbs. The major lines here are the JR Chuo-Sobu, Yamanote and Saikyo lines, the Toei Shinjuku, Oedo and Marunouchi subway lines, and private lines operated by Odakyu, Keio and Seibu Shinjuku. **Where to Eat** Shinjuku is a much better bet for lunch than Akihabara as there is a wide range of good options everywhere you go, whether in the department store food floors or along the main shopping streets. For dinner and drinks, you could head to Kabuki-cho or Shin Okubo for a great selection of Asian cuisines (see main text), or you could go high-end on the west side of Shinjuku with the restaurants and bars in hotels like the Park Hyatt (page 61).

See pull-out map F9-10

EXPLORING
ROPPONGI
Tokyo at its most international

When billionaire construction tycoon Minoru Mori embarked on building the **Roppongi Hills** complex in 2000, he lit the fuse for a spectacular transformation. The opening of the multi-billion dollar urban redevelopment and its combination of five-star hotel, sleek office space, luxury apartments, cinema, art galleries, restaurants, shops, cafés and bars three years later signaled the end of Roppongi's days as primarily a late night destination for drinkers, clubbers, restaurant-goers or anyone looking for some no-strings-attached company. Roppongi had taken a giant step toward becoming one of Tokyo's most cosmopolitan and sophisticated addresses.

Mori's city within a city (see more about Roppongi Hills on page 18, Tokyo's 'Don't Miss' Sights) was soon followed in 2007 by another groundbreaking redevelopment project. This time it was Mitsui Fudosan, Japan's largest real estate developer, and its **Tokyo Midtown** complex (see more on that also on page 18), rivalling Roppongi Hills with its own skyscrapers, five-star hotel, international restaurants, overseas boutiques, bars, galleries and more. Roppongi had always had an international vibe to it because of its nightlife and its location close to numerous embassies, international businesses and international schools, but by the time Midtown had opened its doors Roppongi had cemented a reputation not merely as the place for expats to go and get drunk or find a meal from home but as the focal point of Tokyo's internationally minded community.

In the process of its make-over, Roppongi also became more artistic. That was helped by the magnificent **Mori Art Museum** (Tokyo's Best Galleries and Museums, page 76), now one of the city's premier contemporary art venues, on the 53rd floor of Roppongi Hills, as well as Tokyo Midtown's **Suntory Museum of Art**, known for its collection of traditional Japanese art (www.suntory.com/sma), and the Tadao Ando-Issey Miyake collaboration, the **21_21 Design Sight** gallery (www.2121designsight.jp), which showcases modern Japanese design. Then, across the road from Tokyo Midtown came the cavernous **National Art Center** (page 75, Tokyo's Best Galleries and Museums), designed by Metabolist Movement founder Kisho Kurokawa (who passed away in 2007, the same year the center was opened). If you happen to be in Tokyo in late March, you will be in for an especially good arty treat as Roppongi's major art venues and smaller art spaces combine forces for the annual **Roppongi Art Night** (Tokyo's Best Events and Festivals, page 81), most opening through the night as art happenings take place all over Roppongi.

As for the **nightlife**, that's still there. Roppongi is home to numerous nightclubs and bars, from places to see and

21_21 Design Sight gallery

National Art Center

be seen to some of the city's worst meat markets (check out the excellent bilingual listing site Time Out Tokyo to find out where and where not to go: www.timeout.jp/en/tokyo). And, as it always has been, Roppongi is still one of the best places to eat, whether that's at the foreign-friendly high-end **restaurants** at the Grand Hyatt (http://tokyo.grand.hyatt.jp) and Ritz-Carlton (Tokyo's Best Hotels, page 60), at the many eateries (covering almost all but the tightest budget) in Midtown and Hills, or at some of the hundreds of restaurants out on the streets of Roppongi proper, such as the fine *sushi* at **Fukuzushi**, the theatrically served rustic fare at **Inakaya**, or the exquisite tofu courses served at **Tofuya Ukai** in the shadow of Tokyo Tower (all three covered in the Tokyo's Best Restaurants section, pages 63–6).

The best way to explore the area is to start at Roppongi Hills and its attractions, then head five minutes northwest to the National Art Center, before crossing over Gaien-higashi-dori to Tokyo Midtown. From there, you could also add a little history to your day with a five-minute walk north along Gaien-higashi-dori to take in **Nogi Shrine**, named after Russo-Japan war hero General Nogi Maresuke, who

along with his wife committed suicide upon hearing of the Meiji emperor's death in 1912. The shrine is a modest but peaceful place that tends to come to life on the second Sunday of the month when a flea market is held on the grounds.

With a host of bars and clubs, Roppongi has plenty of options through the night

Time Required A half-day is enough but allow a full day if you plan on taking in all of the art venues. **Getting There** Roppongi Station is on the Hibiya and Oedo subway lines. All the main sights are within a five- to ten-minute walk of the station and are well signposted. To start exploring Roppongi at Roppongi Hills, come out of exit 3 (Oedo Line) or 1C (Hibiya Line). If you end the day at Nogi Shrine, you could also leave the area by Nogizaka Station (Chiyoda Line). **Where to Eat** Both Tokyo Midtown and Roppongi Hills are packed with a good variety of places to stop for lunch, dinner or to pick up a *bento* or coffee and sandwich. For a dinner to remember in Roppongi, check out the Best Restaurants section on pages 64–6.

EXPLORING ODAIBA
Tokyo's best family day out

See pull-out map K13–L15

The man-made island of Odaiba, once part of a series of Edo-era canon batteries built to shore up the defenses of Tokyo Bay against US naval threats in the 1850s, spent much of the 20th century close to disrepair until the Tokyo government chose to expand and transform it into a futuristic commercial and residential district in the late 1980s. What followed was bubble-era spending at its most imprudent. By the mid-1990s, more than 1 trillion yen had been pumped into developing the island and connecting it to the mainland with the construction of the Rainbow Bridge and a new transit system, the Yurikamome Line. Although it took some time before companies and Tokyoites wanted to call the island home, from the late 1990s onward Odaiba finally began to thrive. A major exhibition center—**Tokyo Big**

Sight—was built here, as were offices like the architecturally striking head office of Fuji TV and high-rise condos, but more importantly so too were leisure facilities. Since then, Odaiba has firmly established itself as a family-friendly playground.

For most visitors, a day on Odaiba starts at Shimbashi Station from where the automated Yurikamome Monorail begins a journey that takes it through the skyscrapers of Shiodome, skirting Tokyo Port and then over the nearly 800-meter (2,624-foot)-long **Rainbow Bridge** before reaching the first station on the island, Odaiba-kaihinkoen. Get off here and your day on Odaiba could begin with a stroll around the **Decks Beach mall**, which along with multiple floors of shops and restaurants houses the high-tech **Joypolis indoor amusement park** (page 74, Tokyo's Best Kid-friendly Attractions) and excellent **Legoland Discovery Center** (www.legolanddiscoverycenter. jp/tokyo/en; book online and tickets are much cheaper), which has areas for playing with LEGO, a fun 4D cinema, jungle gyms, several small rides and impressive LEGO-made models of Tokyo and its most recognizable sights. Less interesting, although often with queues coming out the doors, are **Madame Tussauds** and

Rainbow Bridge and Statue of Liberty, Odaiba

the **Trick Art Museum**, while next door is the **Aqua City mall** and near that a replica of the Statue of Liberty overlooking Odaiba's small sandy beach.

Across the road from Aqua City—and on the other side of the Kenzo Tange-designed **Fuji TV building** and its distinctive silver ball—comes the **Diver City Tokyo Plaza** (www.divercity-tokyo.com/en/), which is worth stopping at to see the 18-meter (60-foot)-high statue of Gundam from the *anime* series Mobile Suit Gundam, standing outside. Inside there is also a Gundam theme park.

Back on the Yurikamome (although it's not far to walk between all the sights on Odaiba if the weather is nice), the next stop of note, Telecom Center, gives access to two more of Odaiba's best family attractions, the **Oedo Hot Springs** (Tokyo's 'Don't Miss' Sights, page 19), which combines traditional hot spring bathing, beauty treatments and an Edo-inspired theme park, and the excellent **Museum of Emerging Science and Innovation** (page 73, Tokyo's Best Kid-friendly Attractions); no museum in Tokyo is better geared to kids or has more high-tech hands-on things to play with.

After that, the next station, Aomi, is just as crammed with things to do. **The Palette Town complex** (www.palette-town.com)

Decks Beach mall

here is another mall-amusement park combo, the attractions here including a 113-meter (377-foot) **Ferris Wheel** (the Sky Wheel), the Venus Fort mall, which with Vegas-like "style" is designed to resemble an 18th-century Italian city and palazzo complete with fake sky on the ceiling that changes color during the day, and **Mega Web**, which offers the chance to see and test drive Toyota's latest vehicles as well as showcasing historic Toyota models. By the time you are finished here, you probably won't want to see another mall or indoor amusement park for months, but you will have had a cracking day out.

The Gundam Statue near Diver City

Time Required A full day although you could cherry pick one or two attractions for just a morning or afternoon trip. **Getting There** Unless you are staying in Odaiba (and, to be honest, it's not the most conveniently located base for exploring other parts of Tokyo), go to Shimbashi Station on the JR Keihin Tohoku and Yamanote lines and the Ginza and Asakusa subway lines, and then change to the Yurikamome Line for the Odaiba area. Get off at Odaiba-kaihinkoen Station. **Where to Eat** For lunch and dinner, you will find a range of restaurants and food courts at Decks Beach mall, Aqua City, Diver City Tokyo Plaza, Venus Fort mall and other places in Odaiba, but for something special it's better to head back into central Tokyo, perhaps trying one of the restaurants listed on pages 63–6. **Insider Tip** Actually, two tips. First, Odaiba is much less crowded on weekdays and outside of the main summer school holidays (late July to early Sept). Second, if you are traveling with train-obsessed kids, sit up front on the Yurikamome Line and you can almost pretend to be the driver. The views are excellent, too.

A DAY TRIP TO KAMAKURA
Japan's 13th-century seat of power

See map on page 46

In 1192, **Kamakura** became the power-base for Japan's first shogun, Yoritomo Minamoto. In the 140 years that followed, up until the Emperor Go Daigo wrenched power back to Kyoto in 1333, the town blossomed both as a cultural and political center, leaving behind a rich legacy of temples and shrines that today make Kamakura and its environs one of the most rewarding day trips from Tokyo.

The area's most visited sight, the **Daibutsu (Great Statue of Buddha)**, which is actually located several stations away from Kamakura in the small coastal town of **Hase**, is the best place to start any exploration of the area. So much

history has unfolded during the 750 years the Daibutsu has held court on its stone pedestal at **Kotoku-in Temple**, where he serenely sits crossed-legged, eyes gently closed in meditation. The Muromachi, Momoyama, Edo, Meiji, Taisho and Showa eras have come and gone, as too have numerous wars and natural disasters. In fact, it was because of one of the latter that the Daibutsu is now exposed to the elements as the wooden building that once housed him was washed away by a tsunami in 1495. Yet, other than turning his bronze finish into its distinctive streaky mix of gray, green and soft metallic blue, the years exposed to the sun, wind and rain have been kind to the Daibutsu. The only real damage he might have suffered is losing the gold leaf coating that some believe he may have had upon completion in 1252.

Though tourists primarily come to Hase to see the giant Buddha, other parts of the town are also worth exploring before heading to Kamakura proper. **Hase-dera**, a temple high on the hillside between Kotoku-in and Hase Station,

The Daibutsu at Kotoku-in Temple in Hase

contains a 9-meter (30-foot)-tall gold leaf-covered wooden statue of Kannon, said to have washed ashore at Hase after being carved and tossed into the sea by a monk from Nara during the 8th century. In the opposite direction from Hase Station is **Yuigahama beach**, a peaceful weekday spot with broad ocean views that's ideal for a stroll or a picnic away from Kotoku-in's crowds.

Once finished in Hase, take the Enoden Line back to **Kamakura Station** and head from there to **Kita (North) Kamakura Station** on a longish walk to take in the best of the area's 85 historic temples and shrines. The first major site you'll come across here—at the end of the broad **Wakamiya-oji boulevard** that leads from Sagami Bay and the station area into the heart of Kamakura's temple district—is the majestic **Tsurugaoka Hachiman-gu Shrine** (www.hachiman-gu.or.jp), the entrance of which is marked by a towering, vermillion-lacquered *torii* gateway which, in turn, is followed by a series of humpback bridges leading visitors past two ponds that recall the

violence of Kamakura's "golden years". Designed by the wife of Yoritomo Minamoto, the four islands in the Heike pond are said to be symbolic of the death of Minamoto's enemies (for phonetic reasons the number four is associated with death in Japan), while the three islands in the Gempei pond signify the Chinese character for birth and, with it, Minamoto's victory.

For a glimpse of what life may have looked like back in Morimoto's days, come to Tsurugaoka Hachiman-gu in mid-September for the annual **Reitaisai festival**. As with many shrine festivals, there's classical dancing and parades, food stalls and amusements to enjoy, but making the Reitaisai famous is the **yabusame horseback archery** contest held on the festival's final day. Popular with samurai during the Kamakura period, the contest is a demonstration of both horsemanship and martial artistry in which riders in samurai hunting attire gallop along a straight stretch of track unleashing clinically accurate arrows en route—all done with the measured poise

Tsurugaoka Hachiman-gu Shrine in Kamakura

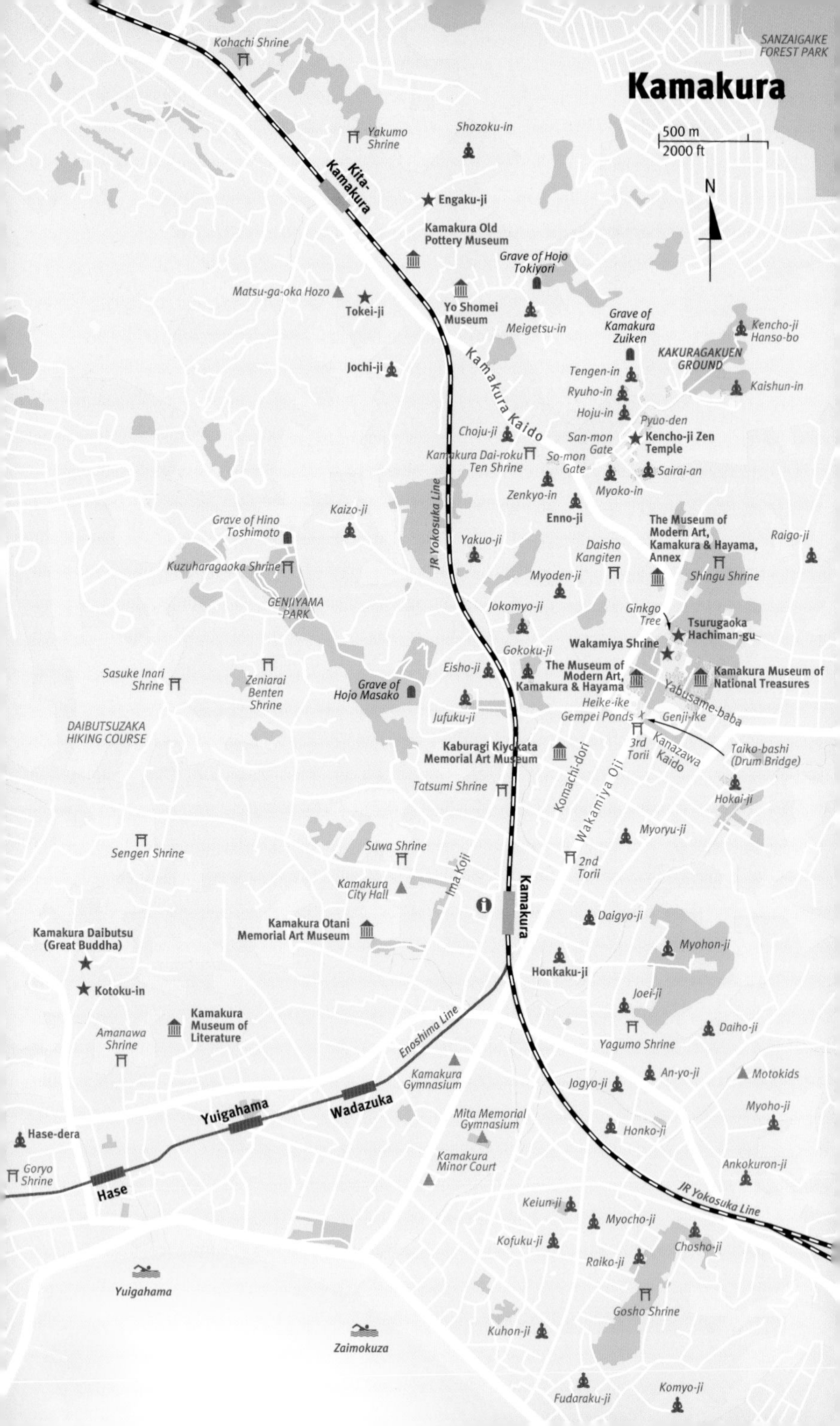

Kamakura

SANZAIGAIKE FOREST PARK

500 m
2000 ft

N

Kohachi Shrine

Kita-Kamakura

Yakumo Shrine

Shozoku-in

★ Engaku-ji

Kamakura Old Pottery Museum

Grave of Hojo Tokiyori

Matsu-ga-oka Hozo

★ Tokei-ji

Yo Shomei Museum

Meigetsu-in

Grave of Kamakura Zuiken

KAKURAGAKUEN GROUND

Kencho-ji Hanso-bo

Kamakura Kaido

Jochi-ji

Tengen-in

Ryuho-in

Hoju-in

Kaishun-in

Choju-ji

Kamakura Dai-roku Ten Shrine

San-mon Gate

So-mon Gate

Pyuo-den

★ Kencho-ji Zen Temple

JR Yokosuka Line

Zenkyo-in

Myoko-in

Sairai-an

Kaizo-ji

Enno-ji

Grave of Hino Toshimoto

Yakuo-ji

Daisho Kangiten

The Museum of Modern Art, Kamakura & Hayama, Annex

Raigo-ji

Kuzuharagaoka Shrine

Myoden-ji

Shingu Shrine

GENJIYAMA PARK

Jokomyo-ji

Gokoku-ji

Ginkgo Tree

Tsurugaoka Hachiman-gu

Wakamiya Shrine

Sasuke Inari Shrine

Zeniarai Benten Shrine

Grave of Hojo Masako

Eisho-ji

The Museum of Modern Art, Kamakura & Hayama

Kamakura Museum of National Treasures

Yabusame-baba

DAIBUTSUZAKA HIKING COURSE

Jufuku-ji

Heike-ike

Gempei Ponds

Genji-ike

Kaburagi Kiyokata Memorial Art Museum

3rd Torii

Taiko-bashi (Drum Bridge)

Tatsumi Shrine

Komachi-dori

Kanazawa Kaido

Hokai-ji

Sengen Shrine

Suwa Shrine

Iha Koji

Wakamiya Oji

Myoryu-ji

Kamakura

Kamakura City Hall

2nd Torii

Kamakura Daibutsu (Great Buddha)

Kamakura Otani Memorial Art Museum

Daigyo-ji

★ Kotoku-in

Honkaku-ji

Myohon-ji

Enoshima Line

Amanawa Shrine

Kamakura Museum of Literature

Joei-ji

Daiho-ji

Yagumo Shrine

Motokids

Kamakura Gymnasium

Jogyo-ji

An-yo-ji

Myoho-ji

Hase-dera

Yuigahama

Wadazuka

Mita Memorial Gymnasium

Honko-ji

Ankokuron-ji

Goryo Shrine

Kamakura Minor Court

JR Yokosuka Line

Hase

Keiun-ji

Myocho-ji

Yuigahama

Kofuku-ji

Raiko-ji

Chosho-ji

Gosho Shrine

Zaimokuza

Kuhon-ji

Komyo-ji

Fudaraku-ji

Kencho-ji Temple

of a Noh performance and the deadly skill and speed of a stealth attack.

Continuing north from Tsurugaoka Hachiman-gu Shrine comes arguably Kamakura's greatest temple, **Kencho-ji** (www.kenchoji.com), the head temple of the Rinzai sect of Buddhism and the country's oldest Zen training monastery. None of the buildings date back to the temple's foundation in 1253, when Kencho-ji was said to comprise an incredible 49 subtemples, yet the current complex still boasts a striking mix of Chinese and Japanese architectural styles that mark it out for special attention. Another 500 meters (1,640 feet) northwest of Kencho-ji, the **Zen temple of Engaku-ji** (www.engakuji.or.jp) has less historic importance than Kencho-ji but is more than a match architecturally, thanks to traditional Chinese Zen design elements and the towering cedars that enshroud the atmospheric complex. The temple is neighbored on opposite sides of Kita Kamakura Station by another Kamakura highlight, **Tokei-ji** (www. tokeiji.com), a 13th-century nunnery-turned-temple that in its earlier years was known as a place of refuge for abused wives. Smaller and more peaceful than Kamakura's more illustrious sites, Tokei-ji is more than anywhere else in Kamakura a fine example of how traditional Japanese sensibilities are so entwined with an appreciation of nature. The temple grounds are decorated by apricot blossom in February, magnolia in March and irises in June, before bush clover takes over in September. It's a lovely place to finish a day out before heading back to Tokyo.

Time Required A full day. **Getting There** Start at Hase Station, which is three stops from Kamakura on the Enoden Line. Kamakura is best reached from Tokyo on the JR Yokosuka Line (via Yokohama) or on the JR Shonan-Shinjuku Line from Shinjuku or Shibuya. From Hase Station, it's a well-marked five-minute walk to the Daibustu. On the way back to Tokyo, use Kita Kamakura Station (nr. Tokei-ji and Engaku-ji), which like Kamakura is served by both the Shonan-Shinjuku and Yokosuka lines. **Where to Eat** Between Hase Station and the Daibutsu there are a few nice cafés and bistros where you can grab a light lunch or an ice cream, but there are more options for lunch around Kamakura Station. **Insider Tip** To varying degrees, the same thing could be said of almost anywhere in and around Tokyo, but visit Kamakura and Hase on a weekday and (save for the possibility of running into school tours) without the crowds you will have much more space and quiet to enjoy the sights.

A DAY TRIP TO YOKOHAMA
A port city steeped in history and overseas influences

See map on page 49

The Yokohama that Commodore Matthew Perry of the US Navy would have seen in 1853, when he sailed his "Black Ships" into Tokyo Bay in a move that essentially forced Japan to open its doors to foreign trade and exchanges after more than 200 years of self-imposed (near) isolation, couldn't be much more removed from the city that greets modern-day visitors. The thriving bayside city was a fishing village with fewer than 100 houses back in the 1850s but now has a population that tops 3.5 million. But that doesn't mean the city has turned its back on its early days. Where Tokyo, bordering Yokohama to the north, is modern and crowded, Yokohama has a more spacious and, in places, more historic feel to it. And although Tokyo is the more cosmopolitan city, Yokohama undoubtedly wears its overseas connections with far more

pride. A day trip here will give you a very different perspective on Japan than staying only in central Tokyo.

A good place to start exploring Yokohama, especially if you plan to arrive around lunchtime, is **Chuka-gai (Chinatown)**, the biggest and arguably most vibrant of Japan's three China-towns, which was established just ten years after Perry first arrived on Japanese shores. The area's colorful streets hold nearly 200 restaurants and 300 shops specializing in everything from Chinese groceries to dumpling steamers, together attracting an estimated 18 million visitors annually.

Just east of Chinatown, a next stop could be the chic **Motomachi** shopping district, defined by smart boutiques and cafés, very different nowadays to its days as the zone where Japanese and foreigners would meet to trade in Yokohama's early years. Nearby, the **Gaijin Bochi** (Foreigner's Cemetery; www.yfgc-japan.com), a graveyard overlooking the bay that looks like it could have been transplanted from any old English village, is another reminder of Yokohama's past.

A few blocks north of the Motomachi and Chinatown area, stretching several kilometers east to west, Yokohama's **harbor front** reveals more remnants of the city's early development. From the pleasant **Yamashita-koen** (park) directly north of Chinatown, the waterfront unfolds eastward starting with the retired passenger liner, the *Hikawa-maru*, which pre-war plied the waters between Yokohama and Seattle, and then continues on to the large **Harbor View Park**, where British troops once had a garrison and which today retains several Western-influenced buildings that date to the late 1800s.

Further east comes the 860-meter (1,500-foot)-long **Yokohama Bay Bridge**,

Chuka-gai (Chinatown)

Central Yokohama

500 m
1 000 ft

N

YOKOHAMA
MINATOMIRAI
SPORTS PARK

MINATOMIRAI

Tide Containing
Pond

SEASIDE PARK
(RINKO PARK)

Yokohama
Harbor

Foresis L

Jackmall East
Media Tower

MM Towers

Otsuka
Kagu

Tsutaya

Foresis R

Leaf
Minatomirai

Keiyu Hospital

Pacifico Yokohama
Exhibition Hall

MINATO MIRAI 21

Seven Eleven

Yokohama
Museum of Art

Tower C

National
Convention Hall

Yokohama
Minatomirai Hall

Yokohama Grand
Intercontinental

Mitsubishi
Minatomirai
Industrial Museum

Mitsubishi

Queen's
East

QUEEN'S
SQUARE

Pan Pacific
Yokohama Bay

Yokohama
Minatomirai
Spa Manyo Club

Tower A

Tower B

Landmark
Plaza

Moku-Moku Waku-Waku
Yokohama Yo-Yo

Ferris Yokohama
Cosmo World

Japanese Overseas
Migration Museum

Japan Coast Guard
Museum Yokohama
Branch

Bank of
Yokohama

Hard Rock

Landmark Tower

JICA Yokohama

Royal
Park

SHINKO PIER

UCHIDACHO

Nippon-Maru

Nisseki
Yokohama
Bldg

Yokohama
Port
Museum

Yokohama
World Porters

SHINKO WARF

Yokohama International
Passenger Terminal

Sakuragicho

Silk Exchange

Navios

Red Brick Park

Blue Line

SAKURAGICHO

Sakuragicho

KITA-NAKADORI

Akarenga

former Bank of
Yokohama Bldg

133

Bashamichi

KAIGANDORI

Toyoko Inn

HONCHO

NYK Maritime Museum

Breeze Bay

NOGECHO

am pm

Marutani

Heiwa Plaza

Kanawaga
Police HQ

Kanagawa Prefectural Museum
of Cultural History

Route Inn
Bashamichi

Yokohama
Customs
Office

Silk Center &
Museum

Legend

Richmond
Bachamichi

OTAMACHI

Autocom
Japan Inc.

MOTOHAMACHO

Yokohama
Archives of
History

Yamashita Park

TAKIWACHO

Comfort
Kannai

Kanagawa
Prefectural
Government

YOSHIDAMACHI

Marinard
Underground SM

Apa
Kannai

Port Opening
Memorial Hall

Port Opening
Square

Center for Int'l
Commerce and
Industry

Kenmin Kaikan
Concert Hall

Toda Peace
Mem. Hall

Drug Store

AOICHO

Nihon-
odori

Continental

Monterey

FUKUTOMICHO

MINATOCHO

NIHON-ODORI

am pm

Yurin-do
Bookshop

Isezaki Mall

Mohan

Yokohama
Chuo YCMA

Urban History Museum

to Gaijin Bochi,
Harbour View Park,
Yokohama Bay Bridge

ISEZAKICHO

Circle K

Yokohama
City Hall

Naka Ward Office

Jal City

Rose

16

HORAICHO

North
Gate

Super
Kannai

YAMASITACHO

Seven
Eleven

HAGOROMOCHO

Seven Eleven

NTT

Zenrin-mon
Gate

East Gate

Chinatown

Seven
Eleven

BANDAICHO

Yokohama
Stadium

Chukagai-dori

Seven Eleven

Toyoko
Inn

Kantei-Byo
Shrine

South Gate

Isezakicho-
jamachi

OKINACHO

Yokohama
Cultural
Gymnasium

Minato-sogo
HS

Yokohama
Central Hospital

Motomachi
Plaza

FUJIMICHO

OGICHO

Yokohama
Sogo HS

West
Gate

Park Square
Yokohama

Motomachi
Shopping
District

Fujimi Jr. HS

KOTOBUKICHO

EIRAKUCHO

MATSUKAGECHO

ISHIKAWACHO

Yokohamayama
Girl's High School

YAMADACHO

CHITOSECHO

Hostel Zen

Seven Eleven

MIYOSHICHO

Sacred Heart
Cathedral Yamate

Motomachi ES

which straddles Tokyo Bay, a beautiful sight when the bridge is illuminated at night.

Head west along the waterfront, however, and Yokohama flexes its more modern muscles, first with **Shinko Island**, a man-made lump of land jutting out into the harbor. Shinko is home to the 107.5-meter (353-foot)-high **Cosmo Clock 21 ferris wheel** and the **Akarenga** (www.yokohama-akarenga.jp), two beautifully renovated redbrick warehouses dating from 1911 that now form part of a chic waterfront entertainment, shopping and dining complex. Beyond Shinko, Yokohama's otherwise fairly low-rise skyline (compared to central Tokyo at least) shoots skyward with modern architectural aplomb in the fashionable **Minato Mirai** area. With the **Minato Mirai 21** (www.minatomirai21.com) waterside development at its heart, this area once occupied by warehouses and dockyards represents Yokohama at its most modern, most notably with the imposing 296-meter (970-foot)-high **Landmark Tower** (www.yokohama-landmark.jp), which for a while after it was built in 1993 was Japan's tallest building. If you fancy ending your day out in Yokohama with a drink and a view, head to the Sky Café on Landmark Tower's 69th floor. The view out over the thriving port city of Yokohama and its bay is out of this world.

Time Required Half a day. **Getting There** Yokohama can be reached from Tokyo Station in 25 minutes on the Tokaido Line and from Shibuya Station in 25 minutes on the Tokyu Toyoko Line. To get to Chinatown, take the Minato-Mirai Line five stops from Yokohama to Motomachi Chuka-gai Station. **Where to Eat** Arrive in Yokohama in time for lunch and Chinatown has dozens upon dozens of good restaurants offering reasonably priced set lunches. If you start early, come the end of the walk, Landmark Tower and the Minato Mirai area also have a good range of restaurants.

Yokohama's waterfront, with Landmark Tower rising above the redeveloped Akarenga warehouses

AN EXCURSION TO NIKKO
Decadently designed World Heritage temples and shrines

See map on pages 52–3

The elaborately decorated buildings that make up Tokugawa Ieyasu's World Heritage-designated Toshogu shrine complex have made Nikko one of Japan's most visited historic destinations for very good reason. But Nikko goes beyond Tosho-gu. Combine Ieyasu's legacy with Nikko's beautiful natural surrounds and the opportunity to stay overnight at one of the area's fine *ryokan* (traditional inn), and Nikko is a must-do on any trip to Japan.

Visitors tend to arrive in Nikko at either of the neighboring **Tobu Nikko Station** or **Nikko Station**, from where the first major attraction is a 20-minute walk or short bus ride away—the much-photographed **Shinkyo Bashi** (get off at the Shinkyo bus stop), a small but striking vermillion bridge above sometimes-foaming waters that was originally built for the exclusive use of *daimyo* and their entourages en route to Tosho-gu. From there, the entourage would have walked to what is now the next stop for many Nikko group tours, **Rinno-ji**, a temple complex of the Tendai sect. Rinno-ji's main hall, the Sanbutsudo, is unfortunately covered for renovation work until 2021, but as the hall's name suggests (lit. Three Buddha Hall) it's the three giant gilded Buddha and Kannon statues inside, not the building itself, that make Rinno-ji worthy of a visit before arriving at Nikko's main attraction.

The decadently designed Tosho-gu shrine complex

Shinkyo Bashi Bridge

And what an attraction. Some 15,000 craftsmen took two years to build the **Tosho-gu** complex, during which they went through some 2.5 million sheets of gold leaf, a fitting decadence perhaps considering that the shrine was built for one of Japanese history's most towering figures—Tokugawa Ieyasu being the warlord who unified Japan at the start of the 17th century to become the first of the Edo-era shoguns. The shrine's Yomei-mon Gate (Sun Blaze Gate) is a riot of color adorned with 400 ornate carvings of dancing maidens, birds and flowers. Its deep red five-story pagoda is accented with intricate decorations and vivid golds and greens. The more serene white and gold of the Kara-mon Gate provides the backdrop for some even more elaborate carvings.

The whole complex is grand and garish in equal measures, yet Tosho-gu isn't entirely about Edo-era ostentation. Its natural setting, amid an ancient crypto-meria forest, evokes a sense of calm. And away from the glare of the main shrine buildings, Tosho-gu boasts many subtle points of interest. Above the shrine's sacred stables, which shelter a white imperial horse given to Japan by New Zealand, hangs a famed carving of the **three wise monkeys**—remember

"Hear no evil, Speak no evil, See no evil"?—an image that represents the three main principles of the Tendai sect of Buddhism.

Nearby, en route to Ieyasu's surprisingly plain tomb, is the equally renowned (though so small it's easily missed) 16th- or 17th-century **Nemuri Neko** carving of a sleeping cat. Just as impressive is the **Honji-do**, a small hall that is actually part of a separate temple, not Tosho-gu. The hall's ceiling is adorned with the painting of a raging dragon that the temple's priests bring to life by standing directly under its head and clapping two blocks of wood together, creating an echo that shrieks through the temple.

If after all that you still have the energy for one more religious site, head next to **Futarasan Shrine** (www.shinkyo.net), a short walk west. Far easier on the eye than Tosho-gu, with its understated design, the shrine is a calming place to take a break, either sipping *matcha* green tea at its **traditional teahouse** or strolling through its **peaceful garden**.

If you are staying overnight in Nikko, then there are more attractions further afield of Tosho-gu worth exploring. A 45-minute bus ride from the main shrine area, **Lake Chuzenji** at the base of the volcanic **Mount Nantei** is a lovely spot for boating, fishing and lakeside walks, especially in fall when the dense mountain woods surrounding the lake turn an earthy palette of reds and yellows. The real draw to Chuzenji, however, are the **Kegon Falls**—the most famed waterfalls in Japan—which cascade 97 meters (318 feet) down a lush, rugged gorge situated a few hundred meters east of the lake.

Nikko Accommodation

Most people staying overnight in Nikko will do so at a *ryokan*, a traditional Japanese inn, which typically combines a fine, seasonal multi-course dinner, tatami mat rooms with sliding paper screen doors and futon, and (alongside all the usual in-room bathing facilities) traditional communal indoor and outdoor hot spring baths. You can find lots of

ryokan options on booking sites like Rakuten Travel (www.travel.rakuten.com) and Japanican (www.japanican.com), while the Japan Ryokan Associtaion (www.ryokan.or.jp) is worth a visit to read about inn etiquette.

Time Required Possible as a very long day trip but better as an overnight trip. **Getting There** Nikko Station can be reached on the Tobu Line from Asakusa in Tokyo in about two hours. From there, frequent buses make the short run to Tosho-gu and Shinkyo Bashi and the longer haul to Chuzen-ji. **Where to Eat** For lunch, there are options around the station when you arrive, and more on the walk between the station and Shinkyo Bashi. One of the most well-known is Hippari Dako, a casual *yakitori* (grilled chicken) restaurant a few hundred meters before reaching Shinkyo Bashi (it will be on your left when walking from the station and has an English sign). Besides the *yakitori*, they also serve up simple dishes such as curry and rice and fried noodles (*yaki soba*). In the shrine and temple complexes, you will also be able to pick up snacks. **Insider Tip** Admission to Tosho-gu costs ¥1,300 but to see all of Nikko's main attractions it's better to buy a ¥1,000 combination ticket permitting entrance to Tosho-gu (Ieyasu's tomb then costs an additional ¥520) and the nearby Futarasan and Rinno-ji temples. All are open from 8 a.m. to at least 4 p.m. See Nikko Tourist Association: www.nikko-jp.org.

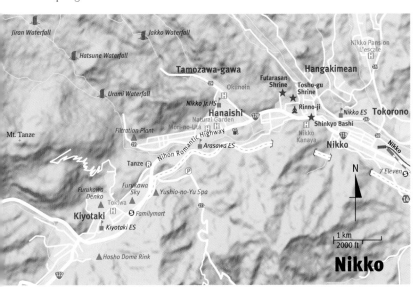

AN EXCURSION TO HAKONE AND MOUNT FUJI
Get up close to Japan's most iconic natural landmark

See map on pages 56–7

With its natural hot springs, stunning mountain and lakeside scenery and proximity to Mount Fuji, Hakone has become one of the most popular weekend escapes for Tokyoites, who come for either an attraction-packed day trip or a more relaxing overnight break that takes them through a well-worn but nonetheless extremely worthwhile sightseeing route.

That classic route begins at **Hakone-Yumoto Station** with a ride on the charming, if not rickety, **Hakone-Tozan switchback railway**. The two-carriage train winds its way upward through a succession of tiny stations before terminating at the mountain village of **Gora**, en route passing through Chokoku-no-Mori Station, which gives access to the

fantastic **Hakone Open-Air Museum**. With more than 120 works displayed across 70,000 square meters (84,000 square yards) of scenic grounds, plus five exhibition halls that include a pavilion home to more than 300 Picasso pieces, it's well worth hopping off the Hakone-Tozan for a couple of hours here. The outdoor work includes pieces from sculptors such as Bourdelle, Rodin, Miro and Moore. In fact, the OAM has the world's largest Henry Moore collection, with 26 pieces on a rotated exhibition schedule. Adding a soothing quirk to a visit, the museum also has an outdoor foot bath where you can stop and soak your feet in natural hot spring water (www.hakone-oam.or.jp).

From **Gora**, a funicular train whips travelers up to the 800-meter (2,625-foot) **Mount Soun** (Sounzan), from where another change of transportation sees them in a cable car being carried over Hakone's mountain ranges to the volcanic valley of **Owakudani** (www.owakudani.com), where the steam rising from sulfur vents and bubbling hot spring pools in the barren lunar valley create a wonderfully eerie atmosphere. The hot

The Hakone-Tozan switchback railway

Hakone Open-Air Museum

springs here are used to cook Owaku-dani's trademark **kuro-tamago**, boiled eggs blackened from cooking which legend says add seven years to the lives of anyone who eats one; the foul stench and almost as foul flavor is a small thing to overcome if the legend is true.

Moving away from the sulfur, the cable car eventually ends at **Lake Ashi** (Ashi-no-ko), where many travelers hop straight onto one of the mock galleons that cruise the lake before later catching a bus back to the Hakone-Yumoto area. Wait for the Disneyesque pirate fleet to move out of sight and the **view of Mount Fuji** set beyond the lake's verdant rim, itself punctuated by the deep red giant *torii* gateway of Hakone Shrine (www.hakone-jinja.or.jp), is one of Hakone's photogenic high points.

Fuji-san, as the mountain is familiarly known, can have an almost hypnotic effect. Maybe it's the way the mountain dominates the vista as it straddles the prefectures of Yamanashi and Shizuoka. At 3,776 meters (12,388 feet), it is comfortably the nation's tallest peak, and with no other mountains nearby Fuji-san stands, skyline to itself, fully visible from sprawling base to narrowing peak. Whatever the allure, the mountain's influence on Japan has been profound. The peak has inspired countless artists and integrated itself into both Shinto and Buddhist traditions. The legendary *ukiyo-e* (woodblock print) printmaker Katsushika Hokusai (1760–1849) was so smitten that he dedicated much of his work to capturing Fuji's changing moods. His woodblock series, *36 Views of Mount Fuji*, includes the iconic *Great Wave Off Kanagawa*, whose snow-capped Fuji in the distance and giant foaming wave menacingly poised to break in the foreground is surely recognizable to anyone with a passing interest in Japan.

In Shintoism, the peak of the now dormant volcano is home to a fire god and—despite its naked lunarscape—a

Mount Fuji and Lake Ashi, not quite as nature intended

The sulfur vents at Owakudani

goddess of trees. In Buddhism, Fuji is home to Dainichi Nyorai, the Buddha of All-Illuminating Wisdom. Consequently, pilgrims have journeyed to Fuji's peak for spiritual enlightenment for centuries. Fuji-san's symbolic power was reputedly recognized even by the Allied authorities in World War II. According to one legend, they planned to bomb Fuji's white cap with blood-red paint in order to break the Japanese spirit.

If you wanted a really close look at Fuji, you could even climb it in the summer months, although it is a long and fairly challenging climb. But you don't need to venture out of Tokyo to get a good view. On a clear day, just head up to the free observation decks on the 45th floor of Tokyo Metropolitan Government Building in Shinjuku (page 38), and Fuji-san reveals all its wonder.

Hakone Accommodation

Like Nikko (page 51), many people visiting Hakone stay overnight at a *ryokan*, a traditional Japanese inn (see page 53 for booking sites), but for an experience bathed in early Western influences on post-Edo Japan, try a night at the Fujiya Hotel (www.fujiyahotel.jp). Opened in 1868 as Japan's first Western-style resort, in its heyday the Fujiya attracted a stream of foreign celebrities and dignitaries.

Charlie Chaplin stayed here. John Lennon, Yoko Ono and son Sean were regulars. The current Emperor and Empress are in

Hakone Area

the guest book, too, while photos of many other illustrious guests adorn the hallways of the Fujiya, which along with the attached *ryokan* (Kikka-so) has Important Cultural Asset status. While the celebs stay elsewhere nowadays, from the high-ceiling dining room where fine French cuisine is served to the bar where Lennon supposedly used to tinkle the piano, the Fujiya still oozes old-world charm.

Time Required Possible as a very busy day trip from Tokyo but much more relaxing as an overnighter. **Getting There** The Hakone area is served by Hakone-Yumoto Station, which is about 90 minutes on the Odakyu Line (using the oddly named Romance Car service) from Shinjuku Station in Tokyo. See Hakone Tourist Information: www. hakone.or.jp. **Where to Eat** Most people staying overnight take breakfast and dinner at their *ryokan* (included in the accommodation fee), and while out and about will stop for something like a simple *teishoku* (lunch set) meal, with options such as udon and soba noodles, *donburi* (bowls of rice topped with anything from tempura to raw fish) and ramen common. The main street in Hakone-Yumoto has a good number of places like this to stop for lunch and you will also find several at most of the main tourist points within Hakone. **Insider Tip** At ¥5,000 the Hakone Free Pass is a great way to cut costs traveling to and in the Hakone area. The pass is issued by Odakyu Railways and covers the train fare to and from Hakone from Shinjuku as well as three days of unlimited use of the Hakone-Tozan line, the Hakone Cable Car and the Hakone Cruise Boat (on Lake Ashi). It also gives discounts at an extensive list of museums, restaurants and shops in the area. For details: www.odakyu.jp/english/freepass/hakone_01

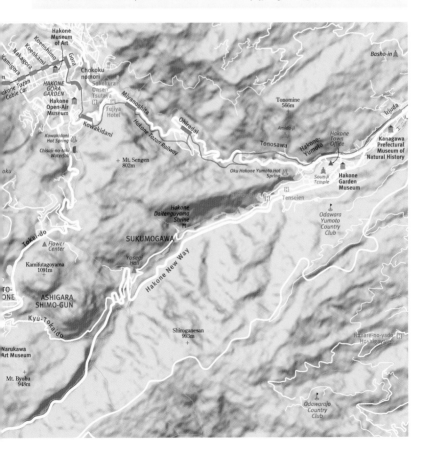

Tokyo's Best Hotels

Mandarin Oriental, Tokyo
The Peninsula Tokyo
The Ritz-Carlton, Tokyo
Park Hyatt Tokyo
Shigetsu Ryokan
Tokyo Ryokan
Grandbell Shibuya
The Claska
The b Roppongi

Tokyo's Best Restaurants

Chanko Nabe at Tomoegata
Monjayaki in Tsukishima
Ramen at Tokyo Ramen Street
Robatayaki at Inakaya
Shabu Shabu at Kisoji
Sushi at Fukuzushi
Sushi on a Budget
Tofu Courses at Tofuya Ukai

Tokyo's Best Nightspots

Club Quattro
Craft Beer Scene
SuperDeluxe
Karaoke
New York Bar
Shin Hinomoto
Womb

Tokyo's Best Shopping

Takeshita-dori
Ginza's Department Stores and
    Boutiques
Omotesando Hills
Shibuya 109
Yodobashi Akiba
MAP Camera at Shinjuku
UNU Farmer's Market
Oedo Antiques Fair
Oriental Bazaar
Nakamise-dori
Kappabashi-dori

Kid-friendly Attractions

Sanrio Puroland
Museum of Emerging Science and
    Innovation
Joypolis
Tokyo Disney Resort
Hanayashiki Amusement Park

Galleries and Museums

Tokyo National Museum
Nezu Museum
National Art Center
Japan Folk Crafts Museum
Shitamachi Museum
Mori Art Museum
Design Festa Gallery

Gardens and Parks

Hama-Rikyu
Kiyosumi Teien
Koishikawa Shokututsu-en
Yoyogi Park
Rikugi-en

Sporting and Outdoor Activities

Adventure Sports
Golf
Hiking
Running
Skiing and Snowboarding
Spectator Sports

Events and Festivals

Roppongi Art Night
Springtime Hanami
Sumidagawa River Fireworks Display
Sanja Festival
Awa Odori Dance Festival
Grand Spring and Autumn Festivals,
    Nikko

CHAPTER 3
AUTHOR'S RECOMMENDATIONS

Where are the best places to stay? What kind of Japanese food to eat? And where? How to make sure the kids have an unforgettable trip? Where to find the most cutting-edge galleries? Which events and festivals to take in? To answer those questions and many more, here are our author's picks for the best of the best in Tokyo.

Tokyo's Kokugikan hosts three 15-day sumo tournaments each year

Senso-ji Temple is the backdrop to numerous festivals

One of Tokyo's 100,000 plus eateries

Hello Kitty at Sanrio Puroland

TOKYO'S **BEST HOTELS**

Places to rest your head from boutique hotel to traditional inns

Whether you want modern five-star luxury or the traditional surrounds of a *ryokan* inn, hipster cool or something that will fit a tight budget, Tokyo's hotel scene delivers all. Here is a run-down of the best of Tokyo's luxury, traditional and boutique hotels, plus some tips on where to book budget options.

LUXURY

Mandarin Oriental, Tokyo

The Mandarin Oriental, Tokyo calls itself a "tower of contemporary luxury" for very good reason. Located on the nine upper floors of a skyscraper in the Nihonbashi neighborhood, close to Tokyo Station and a short hop to Ginza (page 24) in the center of Tokyo, the hotel boasts breathtaking views of the city that reach as far as Mount Fuji on a clear day, a Michelinstarred restaurant, the most indulgent day spa in Tokyo and sumptuously modern rooms. If you were going to max out a credit card for a single night in Tokyo, this would be the place to do it and still have a smile on your face when your bank manager calls.

2-1-1 Nihonbashi Muromachi, Chuo-ku, Tokyo 103-8328, tel. 03-3270-8800. www. mandarinoriental.co.jp

The Peninsula Tokyo

Being located in Yurakucho, just a few minutes' walk from Ginza (page 24) in one direction and the Imperial Palace (page 24) in the other, gives the 24-story Peninsula top marks for location. The fine day spa and elegant interiors do likewise for luxury. The classical afternoon tea served at The Lobby and fine dining mixed with 180-degree views over the Imperial Palace Gardens at Peter are two of the wining and dining options that justify the Peninsula's five-star billing. The Pen doesn't offer up the same kind of chic contemporary luxury of the Mandarin Oriental (above) or Ritz-Carlton (below), but when it comes to classical elegance and refined luxury.

1-8-1 Yurakucho, Chiyoda-ku, Tokyo 100-0006, tel. 03-6270-2888. www.peninsula. com/tokyo

Mandarin Oriental, Tokyo

The Ritz-Carlton, Tokyo

The Ritz-Carlton, Tokyo is everything you would expect of both the brand and its prestigious location on the upper floors of the 53-story Tokyo Midtown urban development (page 18). The 248 rooms and suites blend the contemporary designs of Frank Nicholson with panoramic views of the city that on clear days are accented by Mount Fuji (page 54) to the west. The views from the ESPA-branded spa and the Ritz's highly rated restaurants, one of which was the first Japanese restaurant in a hotel to receive a Michelin star, in 2010, are equally breathtaking. Then there's the location—at Tokyo Midtown and within easy walking distance of Roppongi Hills (page 18), the National Art Center (page 75) and Roppongi's numerous nightlife options. *Tokyo Midtown, 9-7-1 Akasaka, Minato-ku, Tokyo 107-6245, tel. 03-3423-8000. www. ritzcarlton.com*

Park Hyatt Tokyo

Let's get the clichéd bit out of the way first. Located in Shinjuku, this is the hotel where Bill Murray's character Bob stayed and drank in the Sophia Coppola movie *Lost in Translation*. The bar in question, the 53rd-floor New York Bar (page 68), is one of Tokyo's most sophisticated cocktail spots and, like the rest of the Park Hyatt, commands tremendous views across the city center. Next door, the New York Grill is one of Tokyo's best hotel restaurants and comes with a wine collection second to none. As for the rooms, they are an enticing blend of classic and contemporary luxury—think green marble and granite mixed with dark woods—and feature every amenity you would expect in a five-star hotel. *3-7-1-2 Nishi Shinjuku, Shinjuku-ku, Tokyo 163-1055 tel. 03-5322-1234 http://tokyo.park.hyatt.com*

Park Hyatt Tokyo

TRADITIONAL
Shigetsu Ryokan

While Kyoto and hot spring areas such as Nikko and Hakone are known for their *ryokan* (traditional Japanese inns), accommodation in Tokyo, much like the city itself, has become all about modern options. The Shigetsu Ryokan is a very welcome (and affordable) exception to that, boasting warm hospitality, spacious rooms with tatami mat flooring and futon beds, a large communal bath and a restaurant that serves well-presented seasonal cuisine. Within a five-minute walk of all Asakusa's main attractions, including Senso-ji Temple (page 13) and the boarding point for the water bus that plies the Sumida River (page 14), it can also claim a fantastic east-side location. *1-31-11 Asakusa, Taito-ku, tel. 03-3843-2345. www.shigetsu.com*

Tokyo Ryokan

The Tokyo Ryokan in Asakusa is a modern designer's take on the classic *ryokan*, combining traditional elements, such as cedar flooring, *shoji* paper screen doors, *shikkui* walls and paper lanterns, with a modern minimalism and freshness. Like many traditional inns, the shower rooms and toilets are shared with other guests (and they don't supply amenities), but at ¥7,000 for a double room it's still an incredibly good deal in

Tokyo for something with such ambience and so well located.

2-4-8 Nishi-Asakusa, Taito-ku, Tokyo 111-0035, tel. 090-8879-3599. www.tokyoryokan.com

BOUTIQUE
Grandbell Shibuya

Pop art designs in some rooms, warm wooden interiors in others and a selection of chic maisonette suites mark the Grandbell Shibuya out as one of Tokyo's coolest looking hotels (it's a toss-up with The Claska, below). The location is pretty impressive, too, at just a three-minute walk from Shibuya Station—ideal for sampling Tokyo's nightlife. And while the Grandbell isn't for budget travelers, it doesn't have to break the bank. The tiniest of singles start from ¥13,000, doubles ¥22,000, while the sumptuous suites will hit your pocket for a shuddering ¥60,000 a night (OK, the last one might break the bank).

15-17 Sakuragaokacho, Shibuya-ku, Tokyo 150-0031, tel. 03-5457-2681. www.granbellhotel.jp/en/shibuya

The Claska

For a city punctuated by so much cutting-edge contemporary art and design, Tokyo is relatively lacking when it comes to stylish design hotels. The ones Tokyo does have, however, are simply stunning. And the Claska is arguably the best of the lot. Situated in Shibuya Ward, a five minute taxi ride from Meguro Station (the location is the only drawback), the hotel oozes sleekness through every pore, from the contemporary gallery on the 8th floor to the fashionable café-bar and, more importantly, the 16 rooms, which mix traditional Asian and Scandinavian sensibilities to create something distinctly modern and Japanese.

1-3-18 Chuo-cho, Meguro-ku, Tokyo 152-0001, tel. 03-3719-8121. www.claska.com

The b Roppongi

This 76-room boutique hotel lays claim to a prime location—it's an easy walk from Roppongi Crossing, Roppongi Hills, Tokyo Midtown, the National Art Center, the Mori Art Museum and the Suntory Museum of Art—and has a well-priced (¥8,500 for a modern single in this location is a steal) selection of fashionably understated rooms that employ light wood furnishing and neutral color schemes. The only problem might be getting a reservation, but fear not, there are also "b" properties in Akasaka, Ikebukuro, Ochanomizu and Sangenjaya.

3-9-8 Roppongi, Minato-ku, Tokyo 106-0032, tel. 03-5412-0451. www.theb-hotels.com/the-b-roppongi

Business Hotels and Booking Sites

Japan's "business hotels" are a great budget option for travelers who don't want to stay in youth hostels. Nationwide chains **Toyoko Inn** (www.toyoko-inn.com) and **Dormy Inn** (www.hotespa.net) both have English-language booking websites and offer well maintained Western-style rooms with free in-room Wi-Fi or LAN. Toyoko alone has 34 hotels across Tokyo, while Dormy has six, each with its own communal hot spring bath. Prices can vary by location within Tokyo but start from around ¥5,500 for a single and ¥6,900 (per room) for a double. For other budget options, as well as traditional accommodation in places such as Nikko (page 51) and Hakone (page 54), try www.japanican.com, the English-language site of Japan's top travel agency, **JTB**.

TOKYO'S **BEST** **RESTAURANTS**

Sample the flavors that make Tokyo the world's food capital

With more Michelin stars than any other city and restaurants at almost every corner—close to 100,000 licensed eateries in all—it's hard to argue with Tokyo's claim to be the food capital of the world. You'll find every cuisine here, from Korean and Lebanese to burgers and bhajis. More than that, you'll find each and every bit of Japan's wonderful culinary heritage, from *sushi* to *shabu shabu*. In this section are a few of Tokyo's best restaurants, each covering a particular style of Japanese cuisine, plus suggestions for other types of food to look out for.

Chanko Nabe at Tomoegata

There's good reason why sumo images adorn the flags standing outside this always busy restaurant in Ryogoku. Located just a five-minute walk from Japan's main sumo stadium, the Kokugikan, Tomoegata specializes in *chanko nabe*, the hearty stew sumo wrestlers use to bulk up. There's nothing

Chanko nabe

better on a chilly night than picking away at the steaming *chanko* as its simmers along in a big hotpot at the center of your table. And if that isn't enough to make you punch new holes in your belt, they also serve great *sashimi* (raw fish) and other side dishes that wouldn't be out of place in a good *izakaya*. Reservations are essential if you come on the day of a sumo tournament (page 80). Courses range from ¥5,250 to ¥8,400 per person, drinks not included.
2-17-6 Ryogoku, Sumida-ku, tel. 03-3632-5600. www.tomoegata.com

Monjayaki in Tsukishima

Tsukishima, a man-made island reclaimed from Tokyo Bay in the 1890s, is home to one of the Greater Tokyo area's most distinctive dishes—*monjayaki*. Born in the Edo era as a way to make sure nothing went to waste, *monjayaki* comes to the table as a bowl of runny batter mixed with meat or seafood and a variety of finely cut vegetables. It's then fried on a hotplate built into the table until it takes on a consistency not too dissimilar to fried cheese (detractors might say it looks more like vomit!), before you use small metal spatulas to scrape it up and eat directly from the hotplate. Wash it down with a cold beer and also try the *okonomiyaki* (a similar affair but one which resembles a heavy pancake once cooked), which most of the *monjayaki* restaurants also serve. You won't need to worry about reservations, just turn up in Tsukishima at dinner time and walk the aptly named "Monja Street" where you can take your pick of 70 or so *monjayaki* restaurants. *Come out of exit A7 of Tsukishima Station (on the Oedo subway line), cross the small street in front of you and then go straight. Expect to pay ¥1,000–¥2,000 per person, without drinks.*

A restaurant specializing in grilled food, such as stamina-giving *unagi* (eel)

Ramen at Tokyo Ramen Street

You can't come to Japan and not try the noodle that seems to have much of the nation under its spell. Some Japanese will happily queue for hours at the nation's most revered *ramen* joints just for 10 minutes of over-the-top noodle slurping ecstasy. Others will travel hours to sample a regional *ramen* variation. You can skip all that (well, you might need to queue a bit at lunchtime) by heading to Tokyo Ramen Street in the basement of the First Avenue Mall at Tokyo Station. It brings together branches of eight of Tokyo's most renowned *ramen* restaurants, including **Hirugao** (which specializes in noodles in a salt-based soup), **Ramen Mutsumiya** (serving noodles in a *miso*-based soup) and **Menya Shichisai** (where the specialty is *ramen* in a more conventional soy-based soup). Failing that, you'll find *ramen* places all over and most will have a picture menu or, like many other kinds of restaurants, plastic replicas of their dishes on display in the shop window. All you need do is point, wait and then slurp. Alternatively, seek out one of the 25 *ramen* places on Time Out Tokyo's "Best Ramen" list:

www.timeout.jp/en/tokyo/feature/6608/20-Tokyo-ramen-shops-you-have-to-visit. *Tokyo Ramen Street is located on the first basement level of Tokyo Station's First Avenue Mall. www.tokyoeki-1bangai.co.jp/en. Expect to pay around ¥1,000 per person, without drinks.*

Robatayaki at Inakaya

This excellent *robatayaki* restaurant in Roppongi has become a regular fixture in guidebooks and travel brochures. Fine traditional food meets pure theater here. The wooden, rustic interiors and the grilled seafood and skewers of meat make you feel as if you have stopped off for dinner in deepest rural Tohoku, while the way the traditionally dressed waiting staff scream your orders to the chefs, who scream back even more loudly before delivering your food across the counter on the end of a six-foot paddle, could have come straight from the old theaters of Asakusa. Reservations are essential.

5-3-4 Roppongi, Minato-ku, tel. 03-3408-5040. www.roppongiinakaya.jp. Dinner, without drinks, will be in the region of ¥6,000–¥8,000 per person

Shabu Shabu at Kisoji

This 70-year-old restaurant in Akasaka serves *shabu shabu*—thin slices of beef and pork, along with a variety of seasonal vegetables, that you cook in a hotpot at your table then dip in a choice of sauces. What makes this place different to the numerous other *shabu shabu* restaurants around town—besides the fantastic quality of the meat—is that it goes all out on the traditional touches (think tatami mat flooring and ornamental rock garden) to create an incredibly refined experience. Reservations are essential. Courses start from ¥5,500 per person, without drinks, at dinner, but good value lunch sets are also available from ¥1,500.

3-10-4 Akasaka, Minato-ku, tel. 03-3588-0071. www.kisoji.co.jp (to locate Kisoji's other Tokyo branches)

Sushi at Fukuzushi

In business since 1917 and now in the hands of master *sushi* chef George Fukuzawa, Fukuzushi combines everything you'd expect from a traditional Japanese restaurant—impeccable service and hospitality and a beautiful presenta-

Sushi chefs at work

tion of both food and interiors—with modern touches that include a café-bar lounge. All that, of course, would be worthless if the food was not up to scratch. And at Fukuzushi you get *sushi* at its very best, the restaurant sourcing the finest seasonal produce from Hokkaido and serving up delicacies such as melt-in-the mouth *o-toro* (tuna belly cut), *ikura* (salmon roe) that delicately pops on the tongue, and *aji* (horse mackerel) topped with spring onion, *wasabi* and ginger. Reservations are essential. Lunch courses start from ¥2,650 per person, dinner from ¥6,300.

5-7-8 Roppongi, Minato-ku, tel. 03-3402-4115.www.roppongifukuzushi.com

Shabu shabu

Sushi on a Budget

If you can't get a reservation at Fukuzushi or if you don't want to pay for high-end *sushi*, go to the **Tsukiji Fish Market** (page 11) in the morning or at lunch and try one of the many *sushi* restaurants there. You can get a good quality set for in the region of ¥2,000. Even cheaper are *kaiten-zushi* restaurants where you pick plates of low-cost *sushi* that roll past your table or counter on conveyor belts. **The Heirokuzuzhi chain** (www.heiroku.jp) is a good choice and has a branch across the road from the Omotesando Hills mall (page 10). Plates, which usually contain two pieces of *sushi*, start from just ¥130.

Kaiten-zushi (revolving sushi) bars are the most affordable sushi options

Tofu Courses at Tofuya Ukai

This mock Edo-era mansion in the shadow of Tokyo Tower provides the perfect setting for the most exquisitely presented and sublimely flavored tofu-based *kaiseki* cuisine in Tokyo. Taken in tatami mat rooms that overlook a beautifully ornate Japanese garden, the courses here run through multiple small yet sumptuous dishes. You might begin with starters like grilled bamboo shoots served with rape blossoms and sea bream sushi in *sakura* leaves, then progress to creamy tofu blocks simmered in soy milk and deep-fried tofu with sweet *miso* dressing. And it will all be served with the refinement and precision for which Japan is famed. Reservations are essential. Dinner courses, without drinks, range from ¥8,400 to ¥12,600 per person. Lunch courses cost ¥5,500 and ¥6,500 per person.

4-4-13 Shiba-koen, Minato-ku, tel. 03-3436-1028. www.ukai.co.jp

What else to try?

Soba and udon: Japan has many great noodle variations beyond *ramen*. *Soba* (buckwheat) noodles are fantastic when chilled in summer or served in a hot broth. *Udon*, a thick wheat-flour noodle, is also great chilled or in a broth or when used to bulk up a *nabe* (hotpot). You will find *udon* and *soba* everywhere, the cheapest (often under ¥300) being the stand-up *soba* and *udon* places found in and around many train stations.

Yakitori (grilled chicken skewers): The smell of the chicken grilling over coals is one of the best aromas Tokyo's back streets can hit you with. *Yakitori-ya* restaurants, often spilling out into the street, are great for a casual dinner consisting of grilled skewers of various chicken cuts and also vegetables washed down with a few beers. You can find good *yakitori* places under the rail tracks in Yurakucho (box, page 26) and in the back streets of Asakusa (page 31).

Izakaya: These traditional pubs-cum-restaurants are great places to try a wide variety of Japanese food, from simple *edamame* to raw fish served as *sashimi* and deep-fried dishes (*age-mono*) to tofu salads. Every neighborhood has *izakaya* and chain *izakaya* (Shirokiya is a decent one) are ubiquitous, but areas like Asakusa, Shimbashi, Yurakucho (see Shin Hinomoto, page 68) and Shinjuku are especially good hunting grounds.

TOKYO'S BEST NIGHTSPOTS

From clubs to craft beer and karaoke to cocktails

Internationally renowned clubs, intimate live music venues and karaoke are just three options for a night out in Tokyo. Add drinking spots that range from craft beer bars to traditional *izakaya* (pubs-cum-restaurants) and Japan's capital kicks up an almighty storm at night.

Catch a gig at Club Quattro

Club Quattro in Shibuya is a brilliant live venue showcasing an eclectic range of musical genres, from rock to reggae and punk to pop, and an equally varied mix of local artists and overseas acts. Even better is that Quattro is small enough to create the kind of intimate vibe that larger venues just can't buy. If there's nothing that interests you on the bill while you are in town, also look up **Liquid Room** (www.liquidroom.net) in Shibuya and **Shinjuku Loft** (www.loft-prj.co.jp) in Shinjuku.
32-12 Udagawacho, Shibuya-ku, Tokyo 150-0042, tel. 03-3477-8750. www.clubquattro.com

Sample Japan's craft beer scene

You wouldn't know it from the mundane beer choices in most Japanese supermarkets and bars but Japan is going through a craft beer boom. Opened in 2012 by online craft beer retailer Goodbeer, the similarly named **Goodbeer Faucets** in Shibuya is definitely one of the most fashionable bars that have sprung up on the back of the boom. The interiors here

are minimalist, the 40 or so beers (both Japanese and international craft brews) are served from stainless steel draught taps, and the clientele is a mix of expats, salarymen, Shibuya youth and almost all else in between. For a less fashionable but hophead purist alternative, try **Beer Club Popeye** in Ryogoku. Its website is www.40beersontap.com, but it actually has closer to 100 Japanese and international craft beers on tap nowadays under the watchful eye of owner Aoki-san, who having been one of the first to serve craft beer in Tokyo when Popeye opened in 1985 is something of a legend in Japan's craft beer scene.
1-29-1 Shoto, Shibuya-ku, Tokyo 150-0046, tel. 03-3770-5544. http://goodbeerfaucets.jp

Soak up the vibe at SuperDeluxe

SuperDeluxe describes itself best when it calls itself a place for "thinking and drinking". Part-bar, part-club, part-café-bistro, part-gallery and part many other things, this cool venue in the Roppongi area is a hub for Tokyo "creatives". There is always something interesting going on here, whether that's a Pecha Kucha night, local DJs laying down chilled-out grooves, live painting events or when it's simply open as a bar so you can drop buy and try the house Tokyo Ale. Make sure

Tokyo's vibrant nightlife

you check the website before visiting in case it's booked for a private event. *3-2-25 Nishi-Azabu, Minato-ku, Tokyo 106-0031, tel. 03-5412-0515. www.super-deluxe.com*

Sing your lungs out at karaoke

Whether you love the idea of singing in public or loathe it, karaoke is one of those Japanese inventions you really have to try at least once. In Japan, most karaoke places provide private rooms that will sit anywhere between two and a dozen people and in which you sing along to backing music as the lyrics to your song of choice run across a TV screen. While all this is going on, you can pick up an intercom and order food and drink to fuel the fun. Look out for the **Big Echo** chain (http://big-echo.jp) as they have loads of English songs. There's one near The Peninsula hotel (page 60) in Yurakucho (by Hibiya Station, exit 1). If you want a very foreigner-friendly place and don't mind singing in front of an audience, try the expat favorite **Smash Hits** (www.smash-hits.jp) in Hiroo, near Roppongi (page 40, one stop away on the Hibiya Line).

Cocktails and jazz at New York Bar

It's probably about time the **New York Bar** at the Park Hyatt (page 61) in

Side-street eateries and *izakaya* are found all over Tokyo

Shinjuku stopped getting referred to, first and foremost, as the bar in Sophia Coppola's movie *Lost in Translation*. Yes, this is where Bill Murray's morose character would often end his days nursing a Scotch, but the Park Hyatt's main bar has far more to it than a Hollywood connection that grows more slender by the year. For starters, the night views over central Tokyo from way up on the 53rd floor provide a breathtaking backdrop for an evening of sophisticated cocktails and fine cognacs. The wine list includes the largest selection of American wines in Japan. And if jazz is your thing, there are performances from local and international artists every night from 8 p.m. (cover charge applies), with a weekly unplugged session on Sundays. For bigger jazz acts, minus the views, another great option is **Blue Note Tokyo** in Aoyama (www.bluenote.co.jp). *3-7-1-2 Nishi-Shinjuku, Shinjuku-ku, Tokyo 163-1055, tel. 03-5323-3458. http://tokyo.park.hyatt.com/en*

Traditional izakaya Shin Hinomoto

Venues like the New York Bar certainly have their charms but I'm much more of an *izakaya* person. Give me beer and *shochu* over cocktails and lounge music any day. The only problem with *izakaya* (smokiness aside) is that unless you go to one of the mediocre chain *izakaya*, which have picture menus, the best *izakaya* can be impenetrable if you don't speak or read a little Japanese. The problem is solved at **Shin Hinomoto** (aka Andy's Place) in Yurakucho, which is run by Brit Andy, a long-time Tokyo resident. You'll find plenty of classic *izakaya* fare here, from *saké* and *shochu* to *sashimi* and *edamame*, as well as the convivial bordering on boisterous atmosphere that all the best *izakaya* have. The seafood dishes, in particular, for which Andy

After-work drinks

sources fish daily from the nearby Tsukiji Fish Market (page 11), are exceptional. And, of course, Andy is on hand to guide you through the menu choices. It's a very popular place so it's best to call a day or two ahead and book a table.
2-4-4 Yurakucho, Chiyoda-ku, Tokyo 100-0006, tel. 03-3214-8021. www.andysfish. com/Shin-Hinomoto

Dance past dawn at Womb

Most nights you'll get house, techno or electro, and on occasions K-pop might rear its jingle-jangle head. Either way, the massive dance floor, fantastic lighting and sound systems, and line-up of major foreign and local DJs and VJs makes **Womb** in Shibuya one of Tokyo's stand-out clubs. It's easy to see why Mixmag once ranked Womb as one of the "World's Top 10 Killer Clubs". If you want to try another venue as well, check out **Dommune** (www.dommune.com) in Shibuya or the vast **Ageha** (www.ageha. com), further afield in Shin-Kiba.
2-16 Maruyamacho, Shibuya-ku, Tokyo 150-0044, tel. 03-5459-0039. www.womb. co.jp

Where and what else to try?

Elsewhere in the book we've covered drinking options in Shinjuku (in the often quirky bars of Golden Gai, page 39) and included suggestions in the Asakusa section (see **Kamiya Bar**, page 32), but where and what else to try?

Increasingly popular are *tachinomiya* (standing-only bars), where you can get reasonably priced beer, spirits or spirit-based mixes and *saké* along with very simple dishes to nibble on while drinking—almost like a traditional Japanese version of tapas. The back streets neighboring the Ameya Yokocho street market in Ueno (page 33) are a good place to find *tachinomiya*, as are places like Kabuki-cho in Shinjuku (page 38), among many other areas.

As for common Japanese drink choices, most Japanese restaurants, *tachinomiya* and *izakaya* serve a range of *saké* but they also have *shochu*, a clear spirit typically 20–25% (sometimes up to 40%) that's made from either rice, potato or barley and served on ice, straight (the best way, if you ask me) or mixed with water. One particularly refreshing option is the hugely popular *chuhai* (you'll find multiple canned choices in convenience stores, often flavored with fruit), which is *shochu* mixed with soda and perhaps a squeeze of lemon or grapefruit. Beer is also served almost everywhere that has a liquor license, and although most is mass-market lager, there are quite a few good craft brews in Japan, if you know where to look (page 67).

Club, Pub and Restaurant Listings

The above is just a miniscule selection of the best bars, pubs and clubs in Tokyo. For up-to-date news on the hottest clubs, visiting DJs, new bars and restaurants, GLBT venues, music festivals and any other nightlife information you will ever need, visit the excellent **Tokyo Time Out** (www. timeout.jp). You will also find nightlife listings and reviews at the website of the free magazine **Metropolis** (www.metropolis.co.jp).

TOKYO'S BEST SHOPPING

Where to browse, splurge and pick up a bargain

Whether you like brandishing your credit card in brand-name boutiques, hunting for unique souvenirs or rummaging for a bargain at a flea market, Tokyo has shopping options to suit everyone. Here is a run-down on some of the best stores and areas to check out.

FASHION

Takeshita-dori

The narrow Takeshita-dori in Harajuku (page 28) near Harajuku Station adds a youthful contrast to the sophistication of nearby Omotesando-dori (page 27). It's here that you'll find numerous small boutiques catering to teen fashions as well as goth and cosplay tastes. Come on a weekend and the 500-meter (1,640-foot)-long street is so crowded it will take a good 30 minutes to shuffle down it, which gives you plenty of time to soak up the colorful and sometimes quirky fashions.

All sorts of fashions are on show in Shibuya

The main entrance to Takeshita-dori is across the road from Harajuku Station on the JR Yamanote Line and a minute's walk from Meijijingumae Station (exit 2) on the Chiyoda subway line.

Ginza's Department Stores and Boutiques

Ginza (page 24), or "The Ginza" as some of the city's older expats oddly tend to call it, is home to several of Tokyo's most prestigious department stores, with **Mitsukoshi**, **Matsuya**, and **Wako** all within sight from Ginza Crossing. To that you can add a number of sleekly designed flagship stores for a Who's Who of **high-end European brands** (Bulgari, Cartier, Chanel and Tiffany, are the first ones that spring to mind), which have helped cement Ginza's high-cost reputation, but also large branches of affordable fashion brands such as **Gap**, **Zara**, **Muji** and **Uniqlo** that combine to make Ginza a destination for people of all budgets. *Most stores in Ginza are open daily from 10 or 11 a.m. until at least 7 p.m. Ginza Crossing is accessed via exits A1–A10 from Ginza subway station, which is on the Marunouchi and Ginza subway lines.*

Omotesando Hills

Rivaling Ginza as Tokyo's premier high-end shopping area is the kilometer-long main street in Omotesando (pages 10, 27). European brand-name stores line the main drag while small boutiques dot the side streets, but the star attraction—both architecturally and for shopping—is the Tadao Ando-designed **Omotesando Hills** mall, which stretches along almost a third of the street's length. Inside are some 100 restaurants and shops, most of which offer duty free and range from international and local fashion brands, jewelers, bag and shoe stores and lifestyle goods retailers. There are even a few small galleries. If Omotesando Hills whets your appetite for other modern malls, try **Roppongi Hills** and **Tokyo Midtown** (page 18) in Roppongi. *Accessed via Omotesando Station on the Ginza and Hanzomon subway lines. See www.omotesandohills.com*

Shibuya 109

A station away from Harajuku on the Yamanote Line, shopping in Shibuya is also firmly centered on youth. And it doesn't get any more youthful than the eight-storey **Shibuya 109** building. There are more than 100 boutiques here selling all manner of cosmetics, fashions and accessories to hordes of shopaholic young women. Look out for popular brands like the bizarrely named Titty & Co (no, it's not lingerie), Cecil McBee, Egoist and SBY.
A three-minute walk from Shibuya's Hachiko exit, which gives you the chance to cross over the crowded Shibuya Crossing, or right next to exit 6-1. www.shibuya109.jp

ELECTRONICS
Yodobashi Akiba and Akihabara's Electronics Stores

Akihabara's association with electronics began shortly after World War II with the black market trading of radio parts (page 36). Akiba, as it's often called (the Japanese have a habit of shortening place names in casual conversation), has since become Japan's undisputed home electronics capital, with giant department stores such as **Laox**, **Yodobashi** and **Ishimaru Denki** and numerous other smaller stores specialized in electronics parts, robots, used computers and other electrical items. The six-floor **Yodobashi Akiba** (nine floors if you count the restaurants, golf shop and baseball practise nets above it) on the east side of Akiha-

One of Akihabara's many small electrical stores

bara Station is an absolute beast of a store, retailing everything from the latest cameras and kitchen appliances to TVs, audio gear and massage chairs. Allow yourself at least an hour to browse and then head to the fifth floor where you can test out the at times painful massage chairs free of charge. If you are in the Ginza (page 25) and Yurakucho areas, the branch of **Bic Camera** next to Yurakucho Station is just as good.
See www.yodobashi-akiba.com

MAP Camera, Shinjuku

Shinjuku has almost every kind of store you could think of—fine department stores like Isetan and Takashimaya, great sporting goods stores like L-Breathe on Shinjuku Station's southeast side, and giant home electronics stores on the station's west side. But for photographers after the latest Japanese cameras and accessories, MAP Camera is fantastic. Thanks to the habit many camera buffs in Japan have of constantly upgrading and trading in their gear, MAP is the place to find used cameras, lenses and the like in magnificent condition without having to pay full, new price.
See www.mapcamera.com/html/world-guide/english_page.html for a map to the store.

MARKETS

The **Tsukiji Fish Market** and its morning fish auctions are covered on page 11 and the bustling **Ameya Yokocho street market** in Ueno on page 33. Get to both if you can, and also think about checking out the following markets.

Souvenir store on Nakamise-dori

UNU Farmer's Market

Held at the United Nation's University in Omotesando (page 27) every Saturday and Sunday, this farmer's market features stalls selling organic produce, artisanal farm products and handicrafts, but is also a very chilled-out place to grab a healthy lunch. It attracts several dozen great food and drink stalls, ranging from a mobile pizzeria to vegetarian fare. *See www.farmersmarkets.jp*

Oedo Antiques Fair

Found at Tokyo International Forum in Yurakucho on the first and third Sunday of every month (check the website, as sometimes it's held in Yoyogi, too), this lively antiques fair is the largest outdoor event of its kind in Japan, bringing together a good range of fine antiques, curios and bric-a-brac. *See www.antique-market.jp*. A good alternative to this is to stop by the weekly **Sunday flea market at Hanazono Shrine** in Shinjuku. It's smaller but makes for a lot of fun browsing in search of a traditional souvenir.

TRADITIONAL GOODS & SOUVENIRS

Oriental Bazaar

If you only had time to visit one shop to pick up a souvenir, then it would have to be Oriental Bazaar across from Omotesando Hills (page 10). The three floors here have everything from fine kimono and antique furniture to cheap and cheerful T-shirts and sushi-shaped erasers.
See www.orientalbazaar.co.jp

Nakamise-dori

The stalls along Nakamise-dori in front of Senso-ji Temple (page 13) in Asakusa, though in places a bit too touristy, can also throw up some interesting finds, particularly *yukata* (cotton robes) and traditional snacks such as *senbei* (toasted rice crackers) and *manju* (a soft cake with a red-bean paste filling).

Kappabashi-dori

Walk west from Senso-ji in Asakusa, heading toward Ueno, and in about ten minutes you'll come to the wonderful Kappabashi-dori, Tokyo's wholesale shopping district for the restaurant industry. The 170 or so shops here deal in virtuallly every piece of restaurant equipment and kitchen implement imaginable, including some (like **Maizuru**; www.maiduru.co.jp) that specialize in the plastic mock-ups of dishes you'll see in restaurant windows all over town. It's the perfect street for unearthing a culinary (or quirky) souvenir.

Useful Shopping Phrases

How much is (this)? (*Kore*) *wa ikura desu ka?*
Do you accept credit cards? *Kurejitto kaado wa tsukaemasu ka?*
It's too expensive: *Taka sugimasu*
I'll take this: *Kore o kudasai*
Do you have…? *…wa arimasu ka?*
Cash: *Genkin*

TOKYO'S BEST KID-FRIENDLY ATTRACTIONS

Make sure the kids have an unforgettable time in Tokyo

From cool science museums and even cooler arcades to Disney and the home of Hello Kitty, Tokyo has loads of fun lined up for kids. Below are five of the best attractions, while lots more are covered in other sections of the book, such as the Odaiba area (page 42) and Tokyo Skytree (page 12).

Sanrio Puroland

When I first came to Japan and worked for a while as an English teacher, several of my adult students had annual passes for Disney. Minnie Mouse pencil cases and stationary were common in adult classes. Others would turn up with Hello Kitty and Snoopy goods and happily talk of their love for certain cute characters. And while hushed talk in the teacher's room was often of "odd" students, none of the other students in class ever batted an eyelid. It didn't take too long to realize that cute and cartoony in Japan isn't just kids stuff. Sanrio Puroland, the sugary-sweet home of Hello Kitty, is no exception. If you have kids transfixed by anything pink and sparkly, Puroland's mix of Hello Kitty musical revues and dance shows won't disappoint. Neither will the small selection of equally cutesy rides and shops. If you don't have kids, do as the Japanese do and go there anyway. The cute-fest is Japanese kitsch at its finest.

The nearest station is Tama Center Station, 40 minutes from Shinjuku on the Keio Line. See www.puroland.co.jp

Museum of Emerging Science and Innovation

The idea of visiting a museum might horrify some kids, but a trip to the Miraikan (as it's familiarly known) will change that forever. Designed to cater to kids of all ages and all attention spans, the five floors of this high-tech museum are packed with hands-on educational exhibits, covering everything from the International Space Station and extreme environments to life sciences and the human brain. All of them—and this is still something of a rarity in Japan—come with perfect English-language explanations. Before you go, make sure to check the equally well prepared website so you can time your visit with one of the museum's regular demonstrations of cutting-edge tech. Recent ones have

Hello Kitty putting on a show at Sanrio Puroland

included ASIMO humanoid robots and futuristic electricity-powered unicycles. *A five-minute walk from the Fune-no-Kagakukan or Telecom Center stations on the Yurikamome Line. See www.miraikan.jst.go.jp/en*

Joypolis, Tokyo

As someone who grew up playing arcade classics like Commando, Outrun and Street Fighter, I've always had a bit of a soft spot for Japanese arcades. They come in all shapes and sizes in Tokyo, from smoky retro "game centers" where you can join middle-aged gamers reliving 1980s classics to cutting-edge arcades where Japan's games makers flex their creative muscles. Sega's three-story Joypolis indoor amusement park in Odaiba sits at the very top of that latter category. Even die-hard Play Station and X-Box addicts who've grown up with the kind of realistic graphics and smooth game play my chunkily pixilated generation could only dream of, will be wowed by the virtual-reality games, slick car racing cabinets and ear-splitting shoot-em-ups here. *Several minutes' walk from Odaiba-kaihinkoen Station on the Yurikamome Line. See http://tokyo-joypolis.com*

Tokyo Disney Resort

Ever since the "Magic Kingdom" came to Japan in 1983, it's had the country under a spell that Cinderella's Fairy Godmother would be proud of. The resort's two separate amusement parks, **Disneyland** and the more adult-friendly **DisneySea**, attract 14 million visitors annually, making it the third most-visited theme park in the world. Visitors flock in for Disney's trademark colorful parades and big-production stage shows, its mix of white-knuckle rides and fun activities, and plenty of other attractions featuring well-

known Disney characters. The only issue, bar the crowds, is convincing the kids to leave. If you can, come on a weekday outside of the school holidays (the main school vacation is early July through to late August) to avoid the worst of the queues. *Accessed via Maihama Station on the Keiyo Line or by highway bus from Shinjuku. See www.tokyodisneyresort.co.jp*

Hanayashiki Amusement Park

Some would call Hanayashiki in Asakusa (page 32) decrepit, some charmingly retro. I'm firmly in the latter camp. As the oldest amusement park in the country, Hanayashiki's 20 or so old-fashioned attractions are ideal for younger kids yet to have been wooed by the far more fanciful offerings of Disney or Universal Studios. The park's traditional merry-go-round is a timeless attraction, the rickety haunted house is surprisingly eerie and the two-seater helicopters that you can pedal on rails high above the park offer unexpectedly good views of Senso-ji Temple (page 13) and the Tokyo Skytree (page 12). Best of all is the roller coaster, which dating to 1953 is Japan's oldest. It could well be the country's least terrifying, too, given it trundles its way around the park at an almost genteel 40 km/h. *Five minutes on foot from Asakusa Station on the Ginza, Toei Asakusa and Tobu Isesaki lines. See www.hanayashiki.net*

The roller coaster at Hanayashiki

TOKYO'S BEST GALLERIES AND MUSEUMS

Discover traditional crafts, modern art and ancient artifacts

With so many modern art venues and venerable museums, Tokyo could never be accused of lacking cultural attractions. One of the best, the **Edo-Tokyo History Museum**, where you can learn about the capital's development from small fishing village to modern metropolis, is covered in detail in Tokyo's 'Don't Miss' Sights (page 17). On top of that, here is a handful of other stand-out galleries and museums.

Tokyo National Museum

With somewhere in the region of 100,000 artifacts spanning from the Jomon period (14000–300 BC) through to the late 19th century, this giant museum on the northern edge of Ueno Park (page 33) boasts the finest collection of Japanese antiquity in the world. Artistically, the TNM's collection runs from sculpture and paintings to woodblock prints and calligraphy, while ceramics, lacquer ware, textiles, metalwork and arms and armor also get an extensive look in. Give yourself at least a few hours to explore the museum's four main buildings—the Honkan (dedicated to Japanese artifacts), the Heiseikan (archaeology), the Toyokan (focusing on other Asian artworks) and the smaller Gallery of Horyu-ji treasures (home to 300 priceless objects from 7th- and 8th-century Nara).

A seven-minute walk from JR Ueno or Ueno subway stations. See www.tnm.jp

Nezu Museum

The industrialist Kaichiro Nezu (1860–1940) left behind quite an artistic legacy when he bequeathed his personal collection of Japanese and other pre-modern Asian art to be preserved in a museum on the site of his sprawling residence in the Omotesando area (see pages 27–29). Opened in 1941 and more recently given a slick make-over with the addition of a Kengo Kuma-designed building in 2009, the museum's 7,400-piece collection includes seven items designated as National Treasures and nearly 200 more registered as Important Cultural Properties or Important Art Objects. In particular, look out for the folding screen painting "Irises" by the 17th-century artist Ogata Korin and the museum's renowned collection of ancient Chinese bronzes, before heading outside for a stroll around the museum's teahouse-dotted garden and its ponds.

An eight-minute walk from exit A5 of Omotesando Station. See www.nezu-muse. or.jp

National Art Center

The National Art Center in Roppongi (page 40) rightly describes itself as unique and innovative. First, the ultra-modern building is on an unprecedented scale for an art facility in Japan, comprising 14,000 square meters (16,740 square yards) of exhibition space. Second, despite that size, and unlike its sister museums, the National Museum of Modern Art in Kyoto and the National Museum of Modern Art, Tokyo, it doesn't have a permanent collection but instead puts on a variety of exhibitions each year, ranging from Impressionism to retrospectives of Chinese contemporary art.

A five-minute walk from Roppongi Station on the Oedo and Hibiya subway lines. See www.nact.jp/english

Japan Folk Crafts Museum

From Tamba, Karatsu, Imari and Seto ceramics to *katsugi* and *sashiko* kimono from the Tohoku region, the Japan Folk Craft Museum houses a magnificent collection of traditional crafts. There are Ainu costumes and glass beads from Hokkaido in Japan's north, dyed textiles from Okinawa in the far south, and even crafts from other parts of Asia and Europe among the 17,000 pieces on display, while special attention is also given to the Mingei Movement, with work from the likes of Bernard Leach, Shoji Hamada and Kanjiro Kawai.

A seven-minute walk from the west exit of Komaba Todai-mae Station on the Keio Inokashira Line (two stops from Shibuya). www.mingeikan.or.jp/english

Shitamachi Museum

Another Ueno museum, the Shitamachi Museum, gives an insightful look into the history of Tokyo's *shitamachi*—an area of Edo/Tokyo in which the common people lived (page 32). Although it's possible to translate *shitamachi* as "down town", the term originates from the actual level of the land in the area. As the museum explains, in Edo the land to the southeast of what's now the Imperial Palace (then Edo Castle) was lowlands, while to the northwest it was a plateau. As Edo developed from humble fishing town to major city, it was in these lowlands that artisans and merchants lived and it was here that Tokyo's working classes and their *shitamachi* culture took shape. If you want to understand what makes Tokyoites (and especially those from the still proudly *shitamachi* districts of Asakusa, Ueno and Yanesen) what they are, start here.

A five-minute walk from JR Ueno or Ueno subway stations. See www.taitocity.net/taito/shitamachi

Mori Art Museum

Located on the 53rd floor of the sleek Roppongi Hills urban development (page 18), the Mori Art Museum is one of Asia's largest spaces for contemporary art. Its two spacious exhibition areas attract work from a dazzling array of top international and Japanese contemporary artists, previous shows having included a Turner Prize retrospective and exhibitions on contemporary Japanese architecture. The highlights of its 10th anniversay celebrations included a major Warhol retrospective in 2014 and a group exhibition featuring work from artists as diverse as Marc Chagall and Yayoi Kusama. You can combine your visit with Mori's outdoor observation deck.

Located in Roppongi Hills, several minutes walk from Roppongi Station on the Oedo and Hibiya subway lines. See www.mori.art.museum

Design Festa Gallery

This old apartment block turned gallery in the back streets of Harajuku (see box, page 28) is the heartbeat of Tokyo's freestyle art scene. The numerous small exhibition spaces here offer up an ever-changing line-up of art from up-and-coming artists that covers an incredible range of artistic expression, from painting and performance art to photography, video installations and sculpture. In between the exhibition rooms, there's color everywhere; the hallways and walls of DF's laid-back café and *okonomiyaki* restaurant are covered in murals and graffiti, and even the trash cans and drink machines have been blitzed with art. It's youthful, it's fun and it's refreshingly free from pretension. Artistically anything goes here.

A five-minute walk from Meijijingumae subway station or a 10-minute walk from JR Harajuku Station. See www.design-festagallery.com

TOKYO'S BEST PARKS AND GARDENS

Green spaces, traditional landscaping and funky hangouts

Reputation may say otherwise but Tokyo boasts many wonderful gardens and green spaces. Some, like **Shinjuku Gyoen** (page 20) and **Ueno Park** (page 33), are covered elsewhere in this book. Here is the low-down on five more green spaces, from a former shogun's duck hunting grounds to a rockabilly hangout and an immaculate strolling garden.

Hama-Rikyu

Hama-Rikyu Gardens combine with the Shiodome skyline to create one of Tokyo's most striking photo ops, the area's gleaming skyscrapers looming large over the picturesque floating teahouse on the largest of Hama-Rikyu's three seawater ponds. Once the private duck hunting grounds of the Tokugawas, the gardens took several centuries to gradually develop into their current form, a mix of landscaped ponds and rugged fields that bloom with peonies and cosmos. After a morning at the nearby Tsukiji Fish Market for the chaotic tuna auctions (page 11), Hama-Rikyu is an excellent place to catch your breath.

A seven-minute walk from Shiodome Station on the Oedo Line or take the water bus down the Sumida River from Asakusa (page 14). See http://teien.tokyo-park. or.jp/en/hama-rikyu

Kiyosumi Teien

Centered on a large pond with an islet at its heart and landscaped pathways encircling it, this charming garden once belonged to the founder of Mitsubishi, Iwasaki Yataro, who used it as a place for his employees to relax and to entertain visiting dignitaries. Thankfully open to the public nowadays, it's a lovely spot to while away an afternoon, watching people paint and photograph the egrets and turtles that rest on rocks skirting the pond.

A short walk from Kiyosumi-Shirakawa Station on the Oedo and Hanzomon subway lines. See http://teien.tokyo-park. or.jp/en/kiyosumi

Hama-Rikyu's floating teahouse

Koishikawa Shokubutsu-en

Koishikawa Botanical Gardens (Koishi-kawa Shokubutsu-en) in Bunkyo Ward were established by the Tokugawa shogunate in 1684 as a place to grow medicinal herbs. Today, the 16-hectare (40-acre) gardens with arboretum and herbarium, the oldest of their kind in the county, are maintained by the Graduate School of Science at the prestigious University of Tokyo. They contain more than 4,000 species of plants, including different varieties of cherry blossom that make the gardens a great spot for taking in Japan's favorite pink petals when they briefly appear in spring. Better yet, the gardens rarely, if ever, seem to be busy—a benefit of not yet being on the usual tourist trail.

A 10-minute walk from Myogadani Station on the Marunouchi subway line or Hakusan Station on the Mita subway line. See www.bg.s.u-tokyo.ac.jp/koishikawa

Yoyogi Park

Yoyogi Park couldn't offer a more con-trasting view of Tokyo than its neighbor Meiji Jingu Shrine (page 9). Visit on a weekend, when traditional wedding parades might be passing through Meiji Jingu's inner precinct, and Yoyogi Park will counter "old Japan" with groups of rockabillies dancing alongside their Cadillacs and packs of teens posing in gothic dress and *anime* costumes. Venture deeper into the park and you'll probably find a busker or two, playing within earshot of the vendors that keep the picnickers fed and watered, while joggers and cyclists weave around the park's winding leafy pathways.

A short walk from Harajuku Station on the JR Yamanote Line or Yoyogi-koen Station on the Chiyoda subway line. The park is open from dawn till dusk daily.

Rikugi-en

Like the Kiyosumi Gardens (page 77), Rikugi-en near Ikebukuro has a connec-tion with Mitsubishi founder Iwasaki Yataro, having been part of his second residence in the Showa era. This classic garden, however, predates Iwasaki by centuries. Its winding paths, landscaped hills and ornate ponds were created based on 16th-century *waka* poetry themes in the early 1700s by the then shogun's confidante Yanagisawa Yoshiyasu. Come in cherry blossom season and the giant blossom tree near the garden's main entrance is surround-ed by more photographers than the red carpet on Oscar night, but beyond that annual *sakura* frenzy Rikugi-en is as fine a place as any to find a moment of calm and tranquility.

As an alternative to Rikugi-en and Kiyosumi, another classic stroll garden you could try is **Koishikawa Koraku-en** next to Tokyo Dome (http://teien.tokyo-park.or.jp/en/koishikawa). It features some lovely Chinese touches, including a "full moon bridge".

A seven-minute walk from Komagome Station on the Namboku subway line. See http://teien.tokyo-park.or.jp/en/rikugien

Rockabillies in Yoyogi Park

TOKYO'S BEST SPORTING AND OUTDOOR ACTIVITIES

Get a spot of exercise or take in a major sporting event

Take in a game of football or baseball, spend a day watching the sumo or work up a sweat of your own with a round of golf, a run around the Imperial Palace or something more adventurous outside the city.

Adventure Sports

Adventure sports in Tokyo? No, but you can get an adrenalin fix if you head a couple of hours north to the hot spring town of **Minakami** in Gunma Prefecture. There are companies here offering everything from **trekking** to **rock climbing** and **paragliding** to **whitewater rafting**; in fact, there are a dozen or so companies offering rafting alone, including the Kiwi-run Canyons (www.canyons.jp). For more on adventure sports in Minakami, see www.tourism-minakami.com. For elsewhere in Japan, check out www.outdoorjapan.com.

Golf

A decade ago, golf in Japan was still largely the domain of the well heeled and those with corporate memberships. Thankfully, there has been a major shift and the majority of the country's 2,500 or so courses are now open to non-members, many offering very affordable rates, especially on weekdays. Within the Greater Tokyo area there are many well-maintained, challenging courses that cost under ¥10,000 mid-week, with lunch included; many (like the ones I tend to go to in Tochigi and Chiba) can be as low as ¥5,500. As for the golfing experience and etiquette in Japan, it doesn't vary much from golf elsewhere in the world, with perhaps the odd exception that most groups stop for lunch after only playing the front nine (you can forget about a swift 18 holes) and clothing is always formal. Expect a round to take five or six hours. One good course that is well geared to non-Japanese speakers is **Windsor Park Golf and Country Club** (www.wpgcc.com), a couple of hours outside of central Tokyo in Ibaraki Prefecture. To find more (or a driving range in Tokyo), check out Outdoor Japan's www.golf-in-japan.com.

Hiking

Head an hour or two west of central Tokyo and you'll find a good range of day hikes and longer in the **Okutama** and **Tanzawa** areas. The simplest option is to hike up the 599-meter (1,965-foot) **Mount Takao** (page 21), which is only a 50-minute train ride west of Shinjuku. By far the best place to go to plan a hike and get some advice on when to go and what to take, is www.outdoorjapan.com. You could also consider picking up a copy of Lonely Planet's excellent hiking guide to Japan.

Running

One of the city's most popular running routes is the 5-km (3-mile) loop that circles the **Imperial Palace**. Often started near the palace's Sakurada-mon gate (a short walk from Hibiya Station), and run in either direction, it can get busy on weekends but the views of the city and palace grounds are a great backdrop and the route is free of traffic lights and crossings. If you want to change after the

Top-ranked wrestlers parading at the Kokugikan before the afternoon's bouts begin

run, finish the loop at Takebashi Station and head for the lockers and showers at Run Pit on the first floor of Palace Side building (connected to the station; http://runpit.jp/pc). Away from the palace, parks like **Yoyogi** and **Kiba** also have pleasant and mostly shaded running routes, while the banks of major rivers like the **Tamagawa** and **Arakawa** are as flat as a dab and allow you to run without traffic interruptions for hours on end. And if flat isn't your thing, you could even run up and down some of **Mount Takao**'s (page 21) trails.

Skiing and Snowboarding

Tokyo doesn't have any ski resorts of its own but in winter great skiing is surprisingly near at hand. About 80 minutes from Tokyo Station via the *shinkansen*, the town of **Echigo Yuzawa** is a great option, with several well-developed ski and snowboarding fields around the town that offer everything from night skiing to kids slopes and several long runs for advanced skiers/boarders during a season that stretches from around late November/early December to late April/early May. The **Gala Ski Resort** (www.galaresort.jp/winter/english), in particular, is well geared to English-speaking visitors and even has its own *shinkansen* stop. For more information on skiing near Tokyo or further afield, see **Snow Japan** (www.skijapanguide.com).

Spectator Sports

If you prefer your sport with beer and snack in hand, take in one of Japan's major spectator sports—sumo, **baseball** or **J-League football**. There are three 15-day sumo tournaments held annually in Tokyo at the **Kokugikan** in Ryogoku—in January, May and September. Tickets for the day start from around just ¥2,000 and can be bought online via the Japan Sumo Association website (www.sumo.or.jp/eng). Don't plan on getting there early as the top wrestlers won't be fighting (nor the atmosphere rocking) until after 4 p.m. The season for **baseball**, Japan's national pastime, runs from the end of March to early October and even if (like me) baseball isn't your thing, a night at **Tokyo Dome** to watch the Tokyo Giants is a fantastic spectacle. Just watching the choreographed crowd cheering on Japan's most supported (and most loathed) team is entertainment in itself. Schedule and ticket information at the official Nippon Professional Baseball site, www.npb.or.jp/eng. Far better for me would be to catch a **J-League football** game. The season runs from March to December and there are a number of teams based in and around Tokyo. My choice would be to head up to **Saitama** and watch the Urawa Reds at the 60,000-seat Saitama Stadium, which hosted games in the 2002 World Cup. For ticket and schedule details of all J-League teams, see www.j-league.or.jp/eng.

TOKYO'S BEST EVENTS AND FESTIVALS

Traditional dancing, pink picnics, fireworks and more

From art extravaganzas and mid-summer fireworks displays to sweat-drenched dance festivals and centuries-old parades, there's always a festival or major event of some kind going on in Tokyo. With a bit of luck, your time in Tokyo will coincide with one of the great events listed below. If not, make sure to check out the bilingual listings site Time Out Tokyo (www.timeout.jp) or the website of the JNTO (www.jnto.go.jp) before arriving as there will be plenty more good events and festivals you can experience.

Roppongi Art Night

Roppongi Art Night, which has been held in Roppongi (page 40) over one night in late March for the past five years, is like an art-fuelled mardi gras. The self-styled "all-night art banquet" sees all the area's stellar museums and galleries (including the Mori Art Museum, page 76) stay open until dawn, while one-off art installations and ad-hoc galleries appear all over Roppongi. In 2013, the organizers even made the art mobile, with "art boats" driving around town leaving a trail of artistic mayhem in their wake.

If you aren't around for Roppongi Art Night, don't worry. An alternative is the twice yearly **Design Festa**, Asia's largest freestyle art event, which is put together at Tokyo Big Sight in Odaiba (page 42) over two days every May and November by the same people behind the Design Festa Gallery (page 76) in Harajuku. *See www.roppongiartnight.com and www.designfesta.com*

Springtime Hanami

When the annual front of cherry blossoms sweeps northward across Japan in early spring, many parts of Tokyo are fleetingly bathed in a delicate pink. The progress of the nation's favorite petals is tracked on news shows and in weather reports (even in cherry blossom apps nowadays), people staying tuned in to try and time their *hanami* (cherry blossom viewing) parties to coincide with the peak of the *sakura*'s blossom. Some prefer their parties to be more raucous, boozing and singing in the *sakura*'s shade, in places like **Ueno Park** (page 33), which heaves with *hanami* picnickers and party-goers when the buds bloom. Others prefer the more peaceful surrounds of **Shinjuku Gyoen** (page 20), where no-music and no-alcohol rules mean you can enjoy the pink hues as nature intended. Given the choice of just a single *hanami* (although many people do quite a few), however, I'd opt for the **Chidorigafuchi moat** by the Imperial Palace (page 26), taking to the water on a rental row boat and floating under the weeping blossoms. It's the most picturesque cherry blossom site in Tokyo.

Sumidagawa River Fireworks Display

From small local neighborhood shows to extravagant events that bring cities to a near halt, Japan has firework displays going on all over in summer. Illuminating Tokyo's eastern skies on the final Saturday of July, the Sumidagawa Hanabi Taikai is one of the best. With in excess of 20,000 rockets swirling, exploding and painting a rainbow of colors above

The Sanja Festival (Sanja Matsuri) in Asakusa

the **Sumida River** (page 14), the only thing that comes close to the colors in the sky are the vibrant summer *yukata* worn by many in the heaving crowds. If you can't make the Sumidagawa display, the **Tokyo Bay Fireworks** in August (with 12,000 rockets) is another cracker. *See http://sumidagawa-hanabi.com.*

Sanja Festival

Besides perhaps the **Kanda Matsuri** (see page 37), none of Tokyo's spring festivals can beat the Sanja Matsuri. Held in Asakusa (page 31) over the third weekend of May, hundreds of thousands of onlookers fill the streets as hollering teams bounce colorfully decorated portable shrines (*mikoshi*) on their shoulders on a route around Asakusa that takes in Senso-ji Temple and a backdrop of the Sumida River (page 14), the Tokyo Skytree (page 12) and the Philippe Starck-designed Asahi Beer Hall. Alongside the *mikoshi*, the festivities include colorful food stalls and parades of floats on which traditional musicians drive the festivities forward.

Awa Odori Dance Festival

Held annually on the last Saturday and Sunday of August, this offshoot of the ancient Awa Odori dance festival in Tokushima Prefecture, which dates to

1587, sees 12,000 dancers parade through the streets of **Koenji** (six minutes from Shinjuku (page 37), on the JR Chuo Line) performing Awa folk dances. Just don't be fooled by the term "folk"; this isn't bearded men Morris dancing. Instead, the Awa is characterized by irregular steps and an up-tempo rhythm, with colorfully dressed male and female troupes dancing through the streets to an intoxicating mix of drums, flutes, gongs and three-stringed *sanshin*. Best of all, once the official dancing begins to reach its end each day, the Awa descends into a free for all, some of the 1.2 million onlookers joining in with the troupes as side parties kick off all over the neighborhood. A rough translation of the Awa Odori's rallying cry goes, "You are a fool if you dance and a fool if you don't, so you might as well dance." Be prepared to bust some moves. *See http://en.koenji-awaodori.com*

Grand Spring and Autumn Festivals, Nikko

Twice a year, in May (around May 17/18) and October (around October 16/17), Nikko's **Tosho-gu Shrine** (pages 51–2) slips back in time with its near-identical grand festivals. The climax of each of the two-day festivals sees 800 men dressed as Edo-era samurai proceed in file through the Tosho-gu area behind a single portable shrine in a display of pageantry that is believed to have started as a reproduction of the funeral ceremony of Shogun Tokugawa Ieyasu, the man who built Tosho-gu and unified Japan to begin the Edo era. The day before the procession, the festivals also include skillful displays of *yabusame* horseback riding and martial artistry, very much like the **Reitaisai festival** in Kamakura (pages 45–6).

TRAVEL FACTS

The language barrier, the crowds and the cultural differences can all make the prospect of a trip to Japan seem as daunting as it is exciting. They shouldn't. With an efficient and wide-reaching transportation system, well-developed tourism industry and advanced medical services and facilities, visiting Tokyo is by and large safe and straightforward. To help you get the most out of your trip, with the minimum of hassle, we've condensed all the small print you need to know in the following A–Z guide.

Tokyo's JR train map

Ticket machines for the *shinkansen* and express trains

The Tokyo Metro | Taxis are easily found all over central Tokyo

Arriving in Tokyo
VIA NARITA INTERNATIONAL AIRPORT

The majority of inbound travelers arrive at **Narita International Airport**, the main gateway to the country, which is located 60 kilometers (37 miles) east of Tokyo, in Chiba Prefecture. Sadly, getting to and from the airport is a long slog. Despite a faster train connection having been added in 2010, you can still expect to take up to 90 minutes to reach terminal stations in central Tokyo after clearing customs. After that you need to add another 30 minutes to find your bearings among the crowds and get a taxi, bus, subway or train to your hotel.

A good way to get into Tokyo from Narita is to take the **JR Narita Express** train, which runs once or twice hourly at a cost of ¥1,500 (although the fee from Tokyo to Narita is double, ¥3,020) and makes it to Tokyo Station in 56 minutes. An equally good alternative is the Keisei Line, whose **Skyliner service** (2 or 3 hourly; ¥2,470) runs to Nippori in northeast Tokyo in 36 minutes and terminates at Ueno in 41 minutes. Keisei's slower **Access service** (from ¥1,330) connects to **Haneda Airport** in southern Tokyo, on the way stopping at Asakusa (50 minutes) and Nihombashi (58 minutes).

Running more frequently are **Airport Limousine bus services** to Tokyo Station (every 15–30 minutes; ¥3,100; 80 minutes) and the Tokyo City Air Terminal (connected to Suitengumae subway station; every 10–15 minutes; ¥3,000; 55 minutes), although they can run into delays with traffic congestion. **Taxi** fares from Narita to within Tokyo start from ¥16,000 and can be as high as ¥26,500.

VIA HANEDA AIRPORT

Haneda Airport, 15 km (9 miles) south of central Tokyo, is primarily the city's domestic hub but has also seen an increase in international routes in recent years with the opening of a swanky new international terminal in 2010.

From the station in the airport's basement, the **Keihin Kyuku service** runs to JR Shinagawa Station (13–25 minutes; ¥410), from where you can take the Yamanote Line and other lines to numerous destinations. Another option is to take the **Monorail**, which runs to JR Hamamatsucho Station (14 minutes; ¥480), also on the Yamanote Line.

From the airport you can also catch frequent **limousine buses** to various parts of Tokyo, with fares starting from ¥1,000, while a **taxi** will cost around ¥5,000. Both taxis and buses can be affected by traffic congestion but are much easier than the train and monorail if you are traveling with lots of bags. Nothing is worse after a tiring flight than trying to negotiate Tokyo's luggage-unfriendly stations and busy trains with a couple of heavy suitcases.

Calendar of Events

Japan has numerous annual national holidays. While banks, government offices, post offices and many companies close on these dates, most restaurants, shops and tourist attractions will remain open. The main holiday periods are O-bon (a week in mid-August), the New Year holiday (December 30th to January 3rd or 4th) and Golden Week (when multiple national holidays fall between April 29th and May 5th). Be aware that accommodation fees spike during these periods, reservations can be harder to come by and popular sightseeing areas get crowded.

LIST OF JAPAN'S NATIONAL HOLIDAYS

January 1st New Year's Day (Ganjitsu)
January 15th Coming of Age Day
    (Seijin-no-hi)

February 11th National Foundation Day (Kenkoko Kinen-no-hi)
March 20th or 21st Vernal Equinox Day (Shunbun-no-hi)
April 29th Greenery Day (Midori-no-hi)
May 3rd Constitution Memorial Day (Kenpou Kinenbi)
May 4th National People's Day (Kokumin-no-Kyuujitsu)
May 5th Children's Day (Kodomo-no-hi)
September 15th Respect for the Aged Day (Keirou-no-hi)
September 23rd or 24th Autumn Equinox Day (Shuubun-no-hi)
October 10th Sports Day (Taiiku-no-hi)
November 3rd Labor Thanksgiving Day (Kinrou Kansha-no-hi)
December 23rd Emperor's Birthday (Tennou Tanjoubi)

There are many other annual and bi-annual celebrations and festivals that aren't designated as national holidays, and your trip to Tokyo will no doubt coincide with some of them. For more information about these, visit the Japan National Tourism Organization's home page (www.jnto.or.jp) or check out the Events and Festivals section on pages 81–2.

Electricity

The electrical current in eastern Japan, which includes Tokyo, is 100 volts, 50 hz alternating current (AC). Japanese sockets take plugs with two flat pins, so you may need to bring an adaptor. If you travel to western Japan (including Kyoto, Nagoya and Osaka), the electrical current is 100 volts, 60 hz AC.

Embassies in Tokyo

AUSTRALIA
2-1-14 Mita, Minato-ku, Tokyo 108-8361
Tel. 03-5232-4111
www.australia.or.jp

CANADA
7-3-38 Akasaka, Minato-ku, Tokyo 107-8503
Tel. 03-5412-6200
www.canadainternational.gc.ca/japan-japon

NEW ZEALAND
20-40 Kamiya-cho, Shibuya-ku, Tokyo 150-0047
Tel. 03-3467-2271
www.nzembassy.com/japan

UNITED KINGDOM OF GREAT BRITAIN AND NORTHERN IRELAND
1 Ichiban-cho, Chiyoda-ku, Tokyo 102-8381
Tel. 03-5211-1100
www.ukinjapan.fco.gov.uk

UNITED STATES OF AMERICA
1-10-5 Akasaka, Minato-ku, Tokyo 107-8420
Tel. 03-3224-5000
www.japan.usembassy.gov

Coming of Age Day

Traditional *geta* sandals

Etiquette

Make a social faux pas in Japan as a foreigner and most people will smile rather than get upset. Even so, there are some points of etiquette you should make the effort to get right.

- If you get to try a **communal bath** at a traditional inn (*ryokan*), public bathhouse (*sento*) or hot spring (*onsen*), don't get into the bath dirty or soapy. Use the separate wash area near the baths to shower and then rinse well before getting into the communal bathtub, making sure to get in naked and not let your wash cloth enter the water.
- Remove your outdoor **footwear** and change into slippers (which will be prepared for you) whenever you enter a *ryokan* guestroom or someone's house. The same rule applies at many temples, shrines and even certain restaurants and *izakaya*. The best way to judge when shoes aren't allowed is to look out for slippers at the entrance. If there are slippers lined up, use them, then leave your shoes by the entrance or, if available, store them in a foot locker. Once inside, remove your slippers before setting foot on any tatami mat flooring.
- Don't stand **chopsticks** in a bowl of rice or pass anything from chopstick

to chopstick. Both have associations with death and funeral services.
- Good news for fellow cheapskates: **tipping** is not done in Japan. Trying to tip somebody might even cause embarrassment or offense, so you have a ready-made excuse not to even think about doing it.

For a far more comprehensive guide to etiquette, visit the Japan National Tourism Organization's website, www.jnto.or.jp.

For Disabled Travelers

Japan isn't the easiest country to get around for travelers with disabilities. Only a third of the country's train stations are fully accessible and many other public places lack basic facilities such as wheelchair ramps. Although major urban hotels tend to have wheelchair friendly rooms and accessible public areas, *ryokan* and smaller hotels are often lacking such facilities.

Trains have an area in at least one carriage designated for wheelchair users. Station staff can direct you to this and can also be called upon to help wheelchair users get on and off the train using a fold-up ramp they keep in the station office to negotiate the gap between the train and platform. Some stations also have chair lifts to get to and from the platforms.

On the plus side, most newer public buildings and department stores or malls will have barrier-free toilets, access ramps and wide elevators. Many taxi companies also now have cars with chair lifts, though these typically require booking at least an hour in advance.

For a list of accessible hotels and lots of other useful information, visit the Japan Accessible Tourism Center, www.japan-accessible.com/tips.htm.

Getting Around Tokyo

Tokyo has extensive and extremely reliable **train and subway networks**. The two subway systems, Tokyo Metro and Toei, operate numerous lines, while the majority of trains are operated by Japan Railways (JR) and the rest by private rail companies such as Keio and Odakyu. Tickets for trains and subways are sold at vending machines situated near a station's ticket gates, with a signboard above the machine indicating the cost of a ticket to specific stations (sometimes in Japanese only). If you are not sure how much your fare will be, buy the cheapest ticket available (¥130–¥180, depending on the subway or rail company) and then use a "fare adjustment machine" to pay the difference at your destination.

Anyone planning to use the train or subway often should consider buying an electronic **Pasmo** or **Suica pass** (¥500 deposit required), which can be pre-charged with multiples of ¥1,000 and then swiped against scanners on the turnstiles upon entering and leaving a station to automatically deduct the fare. Pasmo (issued by Tokyo Metro) and Suica (issued by JR) can be used on any Toei, JR, Odakyu, Keio or Metro line. They can also be used on certain buses and even in convenience stores and on many vending machines. Tokyo's **bus network** is a nightmare to navigate and is best avoided, but **taxis** can be a handy option. They can be hailed on main streets in most urban areas or found at taxi ranks by most stations. Taxis are metered, with an initial rate of ¥660–¥740 that covers the first two kilometers and then ¥80 charged for each subsequent 275 meters.

Health and Safety

Japan is a fairly safe country. Like the rest of Japan, Tokyo has an advanced medical services infrastructure and there are clinics and hospitals that can treat you in English. Additionally, the drinking water is safe across the country and there are no major insect- or water-borne diseases. Japan also has no requirements for pre-travel inoculation against known diseases.

Over-the-counter **drugs and medications** are widely available at pharmacies, although in most cases the brands will be different to those from home and usage instructions will likely be in Japanese only. It's a good idea to bring a few basic medications with you as a precaution. If you are traveling with a pre-existing condition you should also carry copies of any prescriptions and be sure to bring enough medicine for the duration of your stay. It's also a good idea to carry proof of medical insurance and a note of your blood type and any allergies you have.

If you need to visit a **doctor** during your trip, most major hotels have access to on-call medical services and others will be able to direct you to a nearby hospital or clinic. There are also several **emergency and non-emergency help lines** offering English-language services that can help locate medical care and provide interpretation where necessary (see Useful Telephone Numbers on page 92). All emergency service phone lines can handle English-language calls.

Koban police boxes are handy for directions

Japan has relatively low **crime** rates and incidents of personal robbery or violence are low, but it is still necessary to take basic precautions for personal safety. One potential issue faced by **female travelers** is groping on public transportation. If it happens, scream *chikan* ("groper") and contact the station staff when the train comes to a stop. Alternatively, look for the **women-only carriages** (always the very front or back carriage) now available on most trains and subways during peak travel times.

One danger particular to Japan is **earthquakes**. The country experiences thousands of mostly unfelt tremors annually. While the chances of your visit coinciding with a big quake are slim, it's still worth becoming familiar with escape routes at your hotel and evacuation zones nearby. **If a major earthquake hits, here's what you can do.** Stay away from windows as the glass can splinter and, if you can, draw the curtains or blinds. If you are inside, stay there, taking cover under something sturdy such as a table.

If you have time before taking cover, open any nearby doors to prevent them from jamming and blocking your way out later. If you are outside, go to the nearest open space, such as a park, where you'll be safe from falling objects. In coastal areas, get to high ground as soon as the shaking subsides and stay there; more than 90% of the 18,000 deaths from the March 11, 2011 earthquake were attributed to the subsequent tsunami. As soon as possible after the quake, contact your embassy (see page 85 for embassy contact information).

Heat, too, can be dangerous. Be sure to keep hydrated in summer and take other precautions against **heatstroke**, which sends upward of 50,000 people to hospital every summer in Japan. A hat and a bottle of water are recommended.

Internet

Many Western-style hotels offer free in-room WiFi or broadband access, or failing that will have a terminal or computer in the lobby available free to guests. Those that don't provide free access will often offer a paid service for a daily fee of around ¥1,000. You are far less likely to find Internet access in a *ryokan* or *minshuku*, although some do have a shared terminal or computer available to guests.

Besides hotels, there are also many Internet cafés across Tokyo where you can access a computer for a fee of around ¥200–¥400 per hour. Tourist offices will usually have a list of such places.

Money Matters

The currency of Japan is the yen. The universal symbol is ¥ but sometimes it will be written in the original Japanese, 円, pronounced *en*. Bank notes come in denominations of ¥1,000, ¥2,000 (rarely seen),¥5,000 and ¥10,000. Coins come in ¥1, ¥5 (the only one without Western numerals but recognizable because of the hole in its center), ¥10, ¥50 (also with a hole), ¥100 and ¥500.

Japan is still predominantly a cash society but credit cards are becoming increasingly accepted. Amex, JCB, Visa and Master Card are widely accepted in hotels, restaurants, bars, taxis and shops in Tokyo and other large cities or popular tourist destinations, but it is always advisable to check beforehand. If you head out of Tokyo, make sure to carry ample cash just in case.

Traveler's checks in US, Canadian and Australian dollars, Sterling and Euros can be exchanged at larger banks and at main post offices. ATM at most post offices will also accept foreign-issued cards, including those using Amex, Cirrus, Maestro, Master Card,

Plus and Visa. Seven Bank ATM (found in 7-Eleven convenience stores and some Aeon and Jusco department stores) and Citibank ATM (www.citibank.co.jp) will also take overseas cards. As of writing, ¥100 is worth US$1.

Opening Hours

Although many office workers remain in their offices well after 5 p.m., Japan in most other senses is a 9 to 5 country. **Post offices** tend to stick to a 9 a.m. to 5 p.m. Monday to Friday schedule for most services (though the ATMs often open longer), with main branches operating on shorter hours on weekends. **Banks** are only open on weekdays from 9 a.m. to 3 p.m., although bank ATMs usually remain open until at least 8 p.m., with those in convenience stores open 24/7 year round. **Department stores** and other bigger shops typically open daily from 10 a.m. to 7 or 8 p.m., while **smaller stores** and shops in local areas may stay open later. **Museums** typically close on Mondays (or the following day if Monday falls on a national holiday), but remain open on weekends and national holidays, generally from 9 a.m. to 5 p.m. **Doctors' and dentists'** offices tend to open in the morning, then close for lunch before opening again in the mid afternoon, a typical schedule being 10 a.m. to 1 p.m. and 3.30 p.m. to 7 p.m. With all opening times, remember that banks, government offices, post offices, some tourist offices and many companies close on national holidays, during O-bon and especially during the New Year holiday (see Calendar of Events on page 84).

Useful Japanese

With three different sets of characters (2,136 Chinese *kanji* characters for regular use, and the 48 *hiragana* and 48 *katakana* characters), Japanese at first glance appears to be a very difficult language to grasp. Learning to read and, in particular, write Japanese can indeed take many years. However, given the limited number of vowels and the fixed nature of their pronunciation, it isn't difficult to learn a few useful phrases for your trip.

A BRIEF GUIDE TO PRONUNCIATION

Throughout this book, when referring to place names or Japanese terms, such as Tokyo or Shogun (correctly Toukyou and Shougun), the long vowel has been omitted. In the section that follows, however, long vowels are indicated to give the correct native pronunciation.

Consonants are basically pronounced similarly to English, with the exception that g is always a hard sound (as in **g**et). Vowel sounds work differently, as follows.
a as in c**a**t
e as in r**e**d
i as in ton**i**
o as in h**o**t
u as in p**u**t
ae is two sounds: a (as in c**a**t) and e (as in r**e**d)
ai as in Th**ai**land
ei as in sl**ei**gh
ie is two sounds: i (as in ton**i**) and eh
ue is two sounds: ooh and eh

BASIC PHRASES

Good morning: *Ohayo gozaimasu*
Hello: *Konnichiwa*
Good evening: *Konbanwa*
Good night: *Oyasumi nasai*
Goodbye: *Sayonara*
My name is Smith: *Smith (sumisu) to moshimasu* (polite)/*Smith (sumisu) desu* (informal)
It's nice to meet you: *Hajimemashite*
Yes: *Hai*
No: *Iie*
Please: *Onegai shimasu*

Please (offering something): *Douzo*
You're welcome: *Dou itashimashite*
Thank you: *Doumo* (casual)/*arigato* or *arigatou gozaimasu* (standard)/ *doumo arigatou gozaimasu* (formal)
I understand: *Wakarimashita*
I don't understand: *Wakarimasen*
Excuse me/pardon: *Sumimasen*
Do you speak English? *Eigo wa dekimasu ka?*
How do you say it in Japanese? *Nihongo de nante iimasuka?*
What is this called? *Kore wa nan to iimasuka?*

HEALTH

Hospital: *Byouin*
Doctor: *Isha*
Dentist: *Haisha*
Pharmacy: *Yakkyoku*
Medicine: *Kusuri*
Fever: *Netsu*
Diarrhea: *Geri*
Pain: *Itami*
Cough: *Seki*
Nausea: *Hakike ga suru*
I have a headache/stomachache: *Atama/ Onaka ga itai*
I'm ill: *Byouki desu*
I have a cold: *Kaze ga hikimashita*
I have the flu: *Infuruenza desu*
Food poisoning: *Shoko chuudoku*
I'm allergic to (nuts): *(nattsuu) arerugi desu*
Painkillers: *Chin tsuyaku*
Stomach medicine: *Igusuri*
Antiseptic: *Shoudoku*
Antibiotics: *Kosei busshitsu*

DIRECTIONS

(Excuse me,) where is the toilet? (*Sumimasen,*) *toire wa doko desu ka?*
(Excuse me,) is there a bank near here? (*Sumimasen,*) *chikaku ni ginkou wa arimasu ka?*
Straight ahead: *Masugu*

On the left: *Hidari ni*
On the right: *Migi ni*
Police box: *Koban*
Bank: *Ginkou*
Department store: *Depaato*
Supermarket: *Supaa*
Convenience store: *Conbini*

WINING AND DINING

Do you have an English menu? *Eigo no menyuu ga arimasu ka?*
I would like (some water): (*mizu*) *o onegai shimasu*
Could I have the bill, please? *O-kaikei o onegai shimasu?*
Thank you for the meal (said to staff when leaving a restaurant or to people at your table when finishing your meal): *Gochisosama deshita*

SHOPPING

How much is (this)? (*kore*) *wa ikura desu ka?*
Do you accept credit cards? *Kurejitto kaado wa tsukaemasu ka?*
Cash: *Genkin*
It's too expensive: *Taka sugimasu*
I'll take this: *Kore o kudasai*
Do you have…? … *wa arimasu ka?*

NUMBERS

Counting in Japanese can be challenging. Different systems are used for counting 1 through 10 for different things, and numbers are used in combination with a mind-boggling array of qualifiers. From 11 onwards (thankfully!) there is basically a single set of numbers, though the qualifiers remain equally confusing.

ONE TO TEN FOR OBJECTS

1: *Hitotsu*
2: *Futatsu*
3: *Mittsu*
4: *Yottsu*
5: *Itsutsu*

6: *Muttsu*
7: *Nanatsu*
8: *Yattsu*
9: *Kokonotsu*
10: *Tou*
Example: I'd like two beers, please: *Biiru o futastu kudasai.*

COMMON NUMBERS FOR TIME, QUANTITIES AND MEASUREMENTS

1: *Ichi*
2: *Ni*
3: *San*
4: *Yon* or *Shi*
5: *Go*
6: *Rokku*
7: *Shichi* or *Nana*
8: *Hachi*
9: *Kyuu* or *Ku*
10: *Juu*
11–19: *Juu-ichi, Juu-ni, Juu-san*, etc.
20: *Nijuu*
21–29: *Nijuu-ichi, Nijuu-ni, Nijuu-san*, etc.
30: *Sanjuu*
40: *Yonjuu*
50: *Gojuu*
100: *Hyaku*
1,000: *Sen*
10,000: *Ichi-man*
100,000: *Juu-man*

TRANSPORTATION

Train station: *Eki*
Train: *Densha*
Subway: *Chikatetsu*
Bus: *Basu*
Bus stop: *Basu tei*
Airport: *Kuukou*
Taxi: *Takushii*
Bicycle: *Jitensha*
Ticket: *Kippu*
Ticket office: *Kippu uriba*
One-way: *Katamichi*
Return: *Oufuku*
Window/Aisle seat: *Madogawa/tsurou-gawa no seki*

The Tokyo Metro Marunouchi Line

Non-smoking seat: *Kinen seki*
I want to go to (Ginza): *(Ginza) e ikitai no desu ga.*
Reserved seat: *Shitei seki*
Non-reserved seat: *Jiyuu seki*

MONEY

Bank: *Ginkou*
Foreign exchange: *Gaikoku kawase*
100 yen: *hyaku en*
1,000 yen: *sen en*
10,000 yen: *ichi-man en*
100,000 yen: *juu-man en*

Telephones
PUBLIC PHONES

Most convenience stores and train or subway stations have public phones and you will also find them in many malls, department stores, hotel lobbies and other public spaces. Most public phones accept ¥10 and ¥100 coins and/or phone cards. No change is given if you use a ¥100 coin but unused ¥10 coins will be returned. Prepaid NTT phone cards are available for ¥1,000 from vending machines, kiosks at train stations and convenience stores. To use a public phone, pick up the handset, insert your coin or card and then dial the number.

MOBILE PHONES

You might find that you can use your own mobile phone in Japan if it has a roaming function. However, if you want to rent a mobile phone in Japan, do so upon arrival at the airport as there will be English-speaking staff available to talk you through the rates and rental packages available. Narita and Haneda airports both have phone rental booths.

Useful Telephone Numbers
EMERGENCY AND HEALTH
Police emergency: 110
Police general inquiries: 03-3503-8414
Fire and ambulance: 119
Tokyo Metropolitan Health and Medical Information Center (for help finding English-speaking clinics and hospitals and arranging emergency interpretation): 03-5285-8181
The AMDA International Medical Information Center (emergency and non-emergency medical assistance for non-Japanese speakers): 03-5285-8088 (Tokyo)
Japan Help Line (Toll-free, 24-hour, multilingual emergency assistance service): 0120-461-997

TRANSPORTATION
Narita Airport, flight information: 0476-34-8000
Haneda Airport, flight information: 03-5757-8111
JR East: 03-3423-0111
Tokyo Metro: 03-3941-2004

OTHER
NTT telephone directory service: 03-5295-1010

Time
The whole of Japan operates in a single time zone, which is nine hours ahead of Greenwich Mean Time, 14 hours ahead of Eastern Standard Time and 17 hours ahead of Pacific Standard Time. Japan doesn't observe daylight saving time.

Tourist Offices and Websites
TOKYO
Tokyo Tourist Information Center
1F, Shin-Tokyo Building, 3-3-1 Marunouchi, Chiyoda-ku
Tel. 03-3201-3331
Open daily from 9 a.m. to 5 p.m.
www.jnto.or.jp (main website of the Japan National Tourism Organization)

HANEDA AIRPORT
Haneda Airport International Terminal
2F, 2-6-5 Hanedakuko, Ota-ku
Tel. 03-6428-0653
Open daily from 9 a.m. to 11 p.m.
www.jnto.or.jp (main website of the Japan National Tourism Organization)

NARITA AIRPORT
Narita International Airport
Arrival Floor, Passenger Terminal 2 Building
Tel. 0476-34-5877
Open daily from 9 a.m. to 8 p.m.

HAKONE
Hakone-Yumoto Tourist Information Center
706-35 Yumoto, Hakone-machi, Ashigara-shimo-gun, Kanagawa Prefecture (across the main road from Hakone-Yumoto Station)
Tel. 0460-85-8911
Open daily from 9.30 a.m. to 5.30 p.m.
www.hakonenavi.jp/english/i-info

KAMAKURA
Kamakura City General Tourism Information Center
1F Ekist Kamakura, 1-1-1 Komachi, Kamakura-shi (by the east exit of JR Kamakura Station)
Tel. 0467-22-3350
Open daily 9 a.m. to 5.30 p.m. (until 5 p.m. October–March)
www.kanagawa-kankou.or.jp

NIKKO
Nikko Tourist Information Center
321-1404, 591 Goko-machi Nikko, Tochigi
Tel: 0288-54-2496
Open daily 8.30 a.m. to 5 p.m.
www.nikko-jp.org

YOKOHAMA
Kanagawa Tourist Information Center
1F, Silk Center Building, 1 Yamashita-cho,
Naka-ku, Yokohama City
Tel. 045-681-0007
Open Tuesday to Sunday 10 a.m. to 6 p.m.
www.kanagawa-kankou.or.jp

A *ramen* chef in action

Traveling With Kids
If you are traveling with children young
enough for **push chairs**, it's a good idea
to travel with a chair that is light and
easy to fold away. As many stations don't
have elevators or escalators, you could be
carrying the push chair often. Also bring
a sufficient supply of **diapers**, **baby food**
or any other essential items, as although
Japan has all the items you will need,
you'll likely struggle to find familiar
brands or anything with English-
language packaging.

On **buses**, **trains** and **subways**, children under 6 get to travel free, while kids
aged 6-11 travel half fare. Places such as
museums and **amusement parks** usually offer discounted admission to children, which can be up to a 50% saving
(see page 73 for Japan's most kid-friendly
attractions).

Restaurants often have low-price child
meals available (ask for the *oko sama
setto*; lit. children's set, or *kidozu menyuu*)
and should be able to provide high chairs
and children's cutlery. **Breastfeeding** in
public isn't a taboo but most women tend
to avoid it or do so discreetly. Department
stores always have private breastfeeding
rooms and a place for **changing diapers**,
as do some public buildings.

When booking a **hotel,** it's worthwhile
remembering that Western-style rooms
that can accommodate more than three
people are scarce. Some of the bigger
(and more expensive) international
chains will have large rooms available,
but otherwise Japanese-style *ryokan* or
minshuku, where you get a large *tatami*
mat room that can accommodate lots of
futon, are a great option.

Visas
Any visitor wishing to enter the country
must be in possession of a passport that
will remain valid for the full duration of
their stay. Citizens of Australia, Canada,
Ireland, New Zealand, the UK, the US and
certain other countries, can stay for up to
90 days if they are visiting for business or
vacation. Citizens of Ireland and the UK
can then extend their stay for an additional 90 days while in Japan. Citizens of
other countries will need to leave Japan
and then re-enter to do the same.

If you are a citizen of a country not
mentioned above, you may need to
arrange your visa in advance. For more
information on this or for details of working and longer stay visas, you should
contact your nearest Japanese consulate
or embassy. Details are also available in
English on the website of Japan's Ministry
of Foreign Affairs, www.mofa.go.jp.

INDEX

The Tuttle Story: 'Books to Span the East and West'

Many people are surprised to learn that the world's largest publisher of books on Asia had its humble beginnings in the tiny American state of Vermont. The company's founder, Charles E. Tuttle, belonged to a New England family steeped in publishing.

Immediately after World War II, Tuttle served in Tokyo under General Douglas MacArthur and was tasked with reviving the Japanese publishing industry. He later founded the Charles E. Tuttle Publishing Company, which thrives today as one of the world's leading independent publishers.

Though a Westerner, Tuttle was hugely instrumental in bringing a knowledge of Japan and Asia to a world hungry for information about the East. By the time of his death in 1993, Tuttle had published over 6,000 books on Asian culture, history and art—a legacy honored by the Japanese emperor with the "Order of the Sacred Treasure," the highest tribute Japan can bestow upon a non-Japanese.

With a backlist of 1,500 titles, Tuttle Publishing is more active today than at any time in its past—inspired by Charles Tuttle's core mission to publish fine books to span the East and West and provide a greater understanding of each.

PHOTO CREDITS

000zzz/Dreamstime.com: 83 (left top and middle)

Aaa187/Dreamstime.com: 52

aluxum/istockphoto.com: front cover, 11, 16, 22/3 (middle right), 33, 71

Angela Ostafichuk/Dreamstime.com: 1, 93

aodaodaodaod/Shutterstock.com: 4

CatchaSnap/Shutterstock.com: back cover, 23 (top left), 35

Copycat37/Shutterstock.com: 22 (bottom left), 43 (bottom)

Cowardlion/Dreamstime.com: front cover

cowardlion/Shutterstock.com: 3 (top right)

Det-anan/Shutterstock.com: 28 (top)

fotoVoyager/istockphoto.com: 31, 69

gori910/Photolibrary.jp: 63

Hiro1775/Dreamstime.com: 45

J. Henning Buchholz/Shutterstock.com: back cover, 59 (top right), 80

JNTO: front cover, 44, 87

Jo Chambers/Shutterstock.com: back cover, 7 (left top), 18

JTA/JNTO: 55 (top)

Kitano/Dreamstime.com: 83 (bottom right)

livcool/Shutterstock: 86

Lucian Milasan/Dreamstime.com: 24, 72

Mandarin Oriental, Tokyo: 60

mify/Photolibrary.jp: 7 (left middle), 21

Mike Kwok/Dreamstime.com: 20

Milosz_M/Shutterstock.com: 65 (top right)

Mlenny/istockphoto.com: 67

monocrom-studio/istockphoto.com: 70

Morris G. Simoncelli/JNTO: 76

Nakura_photo/Shutterstock.com: 37

nickfree/istockphoto.com: 68

Nuttapol Noprujikul/Shutterstock.com: 3 (top left)

Oedo Onsen Monogatori: 19

Paolo Gianti/Shutterstock.com: 77

Paylessimages/Photolibrary.jp: 15

Perati Komson/Shutterstock.com: 78

Piya Leelaprad/Dreamstime.com: 59 (bottom right), 73

Pornsak Paewlumfaek/Shutterstock.com: 42

Radzian/Dreamstime.com: 14

Ralph Paprzycki/Dreamstime.com: 38

Rob Goss: 28 (bottom), 74

Sam D'Cruz/123rf.com: 17

Sean Pavone/Dreamstime.com: 5 (bottom), 51, 82

Sean Pavone/Shutterstock.com: front cover, 22/3 (top left), 30, 50

SeanPavonePhoto/istockphoto.com: 36

Simone Matteo Giuseppe Manzoni/ Dreamstime.com: 2

sintaro/istockphoto.com: 65 (bottom left)

Sira Anamwong/Shutterstock.com: 41 (top)

skyearth/Shutterstock.com: 7 (top right), 12

suchi187/123rf.com: front cover, 9

Tawin Mukdharakosa/Shutterstock.com: 34, 59 (middle right)

The Park Hyatt, Tokyo: 61

Tifonimages/Shutterstock.com: 47

tiger_barb/istockphoto.com: 39

TOHO/Photolibrary.jp: 40

Tooykrub/Shutterstock.com: 7 (left bottom), 13, 22 (middle left), 26

tunart/istockphoto.com: 41 (bottom)

tungtopgun/Shutterstock.com: 3 (top middle)

Tupungato/Dreamstime.com: 48, 83 (left bottom), 91

wdeon/Shutterstock.com: 85

winhorse/istockphoto.com: back cover, 27, 29

Xiye/Dreamstime.com: 66

Y. Shimizu/JNTO: 5 (top)

Yasufumi Nishi/JNTO: 43 top

Yuryz/Dreamstime.com: 59 (left bottom), 64

Zybernatic | Dreamstime.com: 56

ムーンライズ/Photolibrary.jp: 10

がんちゃん/Photolibrary.jp: 22/23 (bottom right), 55 (bottom)

源/Photolibrary.jp: 25

せたまる/Photolibrary.jp: 54

Other books of interest from Tuttle Publishing
www.tuttlepublishing.com

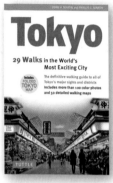

ISBN 978-4-8053-0917-9

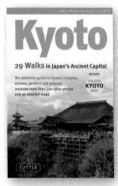

ISBN 978-4-8053-0918-6

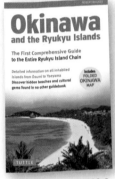

ISBN 978-4-8053-1233-9

ISBN 978

-5

ISBN 97

78-3

13.95   9/15

LONGWOOD PUBLIC LIBRARY
800 Middle Country Road
Middle Island, NY 11953
(631) 924-6400
longwoodlibrary.org

LIBRARY HOURS

Monday-Friday	9:30 a.m. - 9:00 p.m.
Saturday	9:30 a.m. - 5:00 p.m.
Sunday (Sept-June)	1:00 p.m. - 5:00 p.m.